JOHN HOWARD'S
Inside Guide to
PROPERTY DEVELOPMENT & INVESTMENT
for Newcomers

John Howard

Matador
9 Priory Business Park,
Wistow Road, Kibworth Beauchamp,
Leicestershire LE8 0RX
Tel: 0116 279 2299
Email: books@troubador.co.uk
Web: www.troubador.co.uk/matador
Twitter: @matadorbooks

ISBN 978 1789014 785

British Library Cataloguing in Publication Data.
A catalogue record for this book is available from the British Library.

Printed on FSC accredited paper
Printed and bound in Great Britain by 4edge Limited
Typeset in 11pt Cambria by Troubador Publishing Ltd, Leicester, UK

Matador is an imprint of Troubador Publishing Ltd

ACKNOWLEDGEMENTS

This book certainly wouldn't have been written without the help of my mother Betty who, on my 18th birthday, lent me the deposit for my first property deal. She showed great confidence in me and I shall always be eternally grateful to her for that. Thankfully, she also made a good profit!

My bank manager at that time also deserves a mention, for lending me the majority of the money; it certainly wouldn't happen if I was starting my career now.

To the agents, deal finders and others who, over the years, I've traded with, bought from and sold to, I offer thanks.

I would also like to acknowledge my long-term financial backers, who have stuck with me, when I phone up and say things such as "this is one we should be buying", usually doing so without any hesitation.

And finally, to Vanessa Britton with whom I've worked for 25 years on a number of projects, and who has helped me write this book free of charge, having donated her fee to the Aim Higher charity, a school project in Africa for orphans and low-income families, that she set up along with her husband.

CONTENTS

ABOUT THE AUTHOR

John Howard is one of the most experienced property developers in the UK today. He secured his first property deal on his 18th birthday and has gone on to buy and sell 3,500 houses and flats across the UK, in a career that spans 35 years so far.

This gives John a unique insight into the business of property development, coupled with the fact that he is also Director and Shareholder in Auction House UK, the number one property auction business in the country, with over 40 offices across the UK. Along with his partners, John has also recently launched

Exquisite Home, a new estate agency brand, which is to be franchised nationally.

Although his focus is now on developing large schemes, such as his £25m investment made to develop 150 apartments on Ipswich Waterfront, John still loves to buy and sell small sites and properties. He says, "It's great to be down at the coal face, dealing directly with people and doing it all yourself. The problem with the bigger deals is that it's not half as much fun, surrounded with advisors and consultants, so I still much prefer the smaller deals!"

This makes him rare among larger developers who, over time, often completely lose sight of their early years. John definitely has not and, as you will see in this book, he is prepared to pass on tips and advice that have contributed greatly to his success.

Not only will this book help you to make more profit, it will also save you time and money, as he advises you how to avoid common problems and pitfalls that can engulf the novice investor.

INTRODUCTION

The world of property development has changed dramatically over the last 10 years – with buy-to-let mortgages becoming available from building societies, enabling many people to purchase a property for investment purposes. This change has opened up the property market, which, until then, had mainly been dominated by a few private investors with cash available to invest, or property companies and entrepreneurs. These people have seen property as a long-term investment, which over many years, it certainly has been.

Whether you're a seasoned property developer, or a first-time investor, there is always something new you can learn when it comes to property development. It doesn't matter whether you're currently working in property or not. This book is for people who can make decisions! People who want to get on in life, be independent, and increase their net worth, while using their heads rather than their hands!

I've bought and sold many properties, from converting hotels into flats and renovating listed buildings to redeveloping tower blocks and much more in between. I own estate agent offices and am director of the UK's leading residential property auction business, Auction House UK, with over 40 franchises. In this book, I will share my vast experience, because I only wish this book had been around when I clinched my first property deal in my teens!

At one time, I would go to a property auction and know most of the people there. Nowadays, it's a different world, with all sorts of people being able to invest in property, from varying walks of life. Some are inspired, no doubt, by the numerous property TV shows – where the investor spends twice as much as they thought they were going to spend on refurbishment and ends up making a very small profit, if any at all!

Well, the good news is that I'm here to help you avoid those very common mistakes. There is little point spending time and money, only to end up making a very small profit margin at best – and a loss at worst! So, in this book, I'll advise and guide you, helping you to avoid the pitfalls made by many new investors.

I'll explain how to make your money work for you, rather than you working for money. There are many ways to deal, invest in, and develop property. I'll tell you how to find deals and investors. I'll show you how to make your own decisions on what properties will be worth, once refurbished, and not just rely on the estate agent's valuation. I'll go through all the traps that people fall into and how to avoid them, show you how to trade in a rising market and, more importantly, how to get out of a dropping market.

I won't tell you what colour to paint the walls, or which type of brewed coffee smells best in order to help sell your properties. What I will do is give you hard-nosed property advice from someone who's been developing property for 35 years, rather than the opinion of a TV presenter, with no, or hardly any experience in property whatsoever.

This book will help you decide what sort of property investor you want to become, whether it's investing for the long term, or developing property to resell. Either way, it will help you maximise your profits. If you're already investing in property, then you'll sharpen up your game and make your deals more successful than they currently are.

In part 1, we'll look at the basics of how to get started, put a deal together, and fund your deals, plus the basic process of buying and selling. In part 2, we'll go in-depth, looking at which types of property to choose, the types of property development, buying to rent, trading during varying property markets, and how to choose and work with builders, estate agents, and solicitors.

So, let's get started!

PART I:
THE BASICS OF
PROPERTY DEVELOPMENT

CHAPTER 1:
GETTING STARTED

It might sound obvious, but I believe in keeping things as simple as possible when dealing in property. It doesn't matter whether you're thinking about investing, or trading — it's a very simple business and those who forget that, do so at the risk of losing both their sanity and their profit. While I don't wish to offend anyone (don't forget, I'm a property developer myself), I'll go so far as to say that, if someone is too much of an intellectual, they normally don't make a great property person. This is because they tend to overanalyse everything and, as a result, they never get off the starting blocks. So, remember — always keep it simple.

If you're new to property developing, the place to start is most certainly at the beginning, where there are a number of choices to make. You need to decide what you want to do, how much risk you want to take, how quickly you want a return on your investment, and how rich you want to become.

To start with, it's clearly a massive advantage to have another income, be it full or part-time, to subsidise any property dealing, but that's not to say it can't be done on limited funds. Being able to fund your lifestyle away from any property proceeds (the money that comes from the sale of the property), even in the short-term, means you don't have to live off your profits and can therefore reinvest them into your next deal, minus the tax you need to pay of course. Most people who are considering property dealing, or are already buying property, have a full-time job to subsidise such endeavours.

However, if you don't have that luxury and decide you want to concentrate full-time on your property business, as I do, then you need to be highly active. You need to get to know many people, especially those who will buy from you, whether it's before you've paid for the properties, or straight afterwards. You need to buy and sell property *very quickly* to make an income to live off – and to keep the money turning over.

There is also the option that you can act as a **deal finder** for other people. Some people have a full-time job themselves, so don't have the time to seek out deals. Others are just not suited to doing it themselves, whether they have the time or not, so they rely on deal finders to do the job for them. I still find properties for some clients. No one can buy everything they want to buy, so I introduce houses or flats to these people and charge them a 2% finder's fee.

You might also be able to manage people's properties for them, or oversee building work prior to them letting the property out. Perhaps you can turn your hand to decorating, or general building work yourself, in order to raise the necessary funds to purchase your own properties.

You might also find that a part-time job works well alongside these options. I once read about a cleaner who cleaned a bank every night and ended up being worth millions of pounds. As she emptied the waste paper baskets, she was able to glean information on which shares to buy. She invested a small amount to start with, building up gradually until she ended up owning a large share portfolio. And she still carried on working, cleaning the bank every night.

It's worth bearing in mind that even the really well-known property developers and builders in this country started by building or renovating *just one property*. Everyone has to start somewhere, so just make sure your first deal is a good one. You'll discover how to ensure that later in the book.

What to buy?

While there are many areas of property development that should see you following sound commercial principles, deciding what type of property to buy might be your most important *individual* issue. What to buy depends on how much money you have and what is of interest to you personally. There is very little point in doing a job that you're not genuinely suited to, and if you buy a property that doesn't interest you from the start, then it won't keep your focused attention during the project either.

Once you have started developing, you can look to specialise in a field of property that you've found you are comfortable in. When your connections get to know what your specialism is, they will automatically contact you when anything like it comes up.

So, choose property that inspires you. Whether it's buying a house in need of renovation, building up a rental portfolio, or even buying an old vacant shop and letting it out, all are perfectly sound choices. The challenge is usually not finding such properties – it is finding them at the right price in order to make a good profit.

For me, it's always been flats, mainly conversions and, more recently, problem sites, often those without planning permission. One of the reasons for this is that I have a reputation for being able to sort out problems, so banks will lend me money on sites with no planning permission, knowing that I have the ability to sort it out and sell it on for a profit. In Chapter 7, we'll look more in-depth at the types of property you might want to buy.

What type of developer are you?

There are many different types of people who get involved in property development and investment. It's quite common to find builders and estate agents becoming property developers or investors, as they have experience in these fields. However, there are numerous people who become full- or part-time developers, from school teachers and postmen to people who have sold their company and are using the money to invest in property. Everyone is welcome in this field!

I've seen many builders move into property developing, having 'seen the light', deciding to make more money by building new houses themselves, rather than for others. However, the risk for such builders is that they are often craftsmen and are in danger of building 'too' well. This doesn't mean builder-developers should cut corners; however, building to a higher specification than required often leads to higher prices than purchasers want to pay for similar properties. A sensible approach for builder-developers is building to a specification that affords a very **competitive** selling price, as this sees the property sold quickly, meaning the profits can be invested in the next deal.

Estate agents often take up property developing themselves, having worked for an estate agency chain, or independent high-street local agent for a while. Having learnt their craft on the front line, many estate agents make very good property developers, providing they don't believe their own hype! Those who get a little braver and break out of their employed status soon realise that there's a lot more money in buying and selling than there is in taking calls and showing interested purchasers around houses on their company's books.

Personal experience and personality

Any talk of property developers often summons images of gregarious, loud, risk-taking individuals. The truth is often very far removed from this stereotype, especially when it comes to those who are successful. Those who are cautious by nature often make very good property developers, providing they have the confidence to take the plunge when the time and the price is right.

Being cautious isn't a bad thing in itself, especially if you're able to establish an 'out' before you buy 'in'. In other words, always know what you're going to do **before you buy**, even if it doesn't go the way you thought it would during the project. This is often not something that an estate agent or builder would naturally do as, in their own estimation, one can sell anything, and the other builds the best houses ever! Therefore, the 'out' plan is something you may need to work on, if it doesn't come naturally to you.

Being a great property developer is all about finding the middle ground between over-confidence and over-cautiousness. Being over-cautious could result in you never buying anything, as it's very easy to talk yourself out of a deal. What you should be asking yourself is 'What do I do if it goes wrong?' If the answer to that question is feasible and acceptable, then do it.

You may be over-confident because you're an estate agent or builder with experience, and yes, you may well make money, but you do need to practise cautiousness too.

Even if you're not in one of these roles – if you believe in yourself, then you certainly will make money too. If you have experience in any field that is useful to property development, then clearly you should use it to the best of your ability.

Money matters

Having decided what type of property you would like to buy, the next questions to ask yourself are how much you should make out of a first deal and how much you should pay for the property.

Traditionally, the norm was working to a net profit of 25%, after taking every cost into account, including interest. If you ever watch popular TV shows, they all foster the idea that you can do up a house for a pittance and sell it for a fortune. The truth, of course, is very different.

Currently, I am often forced to work to a net profit margin of 20% minimum, having taken into account all the expenses, including solicitors costs, bank interest, and building costs. There is no point in kidding yourself by not accounting for all of these costs; in fact, not doing so is foolhardy and will lead to disappointment. If you aim for a 20% margin, then you may actually do better, but if you do worse, you still shouldn't lose money.

As a property dealer, I'm often asked "Should I set a limit on what I pay for a given property, and if so, how can I arrive at the correct figure?" When going through an estate agent, you have the luxury of time to investigate prices, and this ensures that you offer the right amount of money. It is often said that the right price is the price that the buyer is prepared to pay. In other words, there really is no such thing as the right price!

As a buyer, you can negotiate, and you can also change what you have offered to the seller (also known as a vendor) should any problems arise. The vendor may or may not allow you to do so, but it is a buyer's prerogative. When trying to arrive at an offer price, remember the rule of making a 20% net profit after all costs, including interest.

If you like a property and could see yourself living there, you are likely to be far more biased about what you think it's worth, than if you don't see it as a potential home. However, unless you go bankrupt and have to move into it, whether you would like to live in a property or not is irrelevant. You need to be **objective** to ensure you only pay the true value of the property as an investment proposition. If you want to succeed in property developing, you need to become hard-nosed about it. It is quite simple really. If you can make a minimum 20% net profit, then it really doesn't matter whether you personally like the property or not, so get on and get it bought!

Always be prepared to walk away if the figures don't stack up. If your assessment of the costs leads you to believe that you're not going to make the net profit you expect to, then it's not a good deal. Also, never assume you can get the building work undertaken for cheaper than what you're being told by the builder. In my experience, it always costs more in the end.

Adding value to your property

In order to work out whether you can make a decent profit, you have to calculate all of the costs, but you should always have an eye on **adding value** too. When you're viewing a property for sale, you should be thinking about how you can add extra value to the property over and above refurbishing or renovation, as this can add to your bottom line dramatically.

For instance, if there isn't currently a car parking space and you could create one in the front garden, this could potentially add £20,000+ to a property. If you decide to do this, you may need to seek permission from the council to put in a drop kerb, as it will look strange without one. Also, bear in mind that councils usually have a list of contractors who are allowed to carry out this type of work, and your builder probably won't be on it.

If there is room for a garage to be built, then you might consider it – but be wary, as brick-built garages cost a lot of money to build and not everyone is looking for a garage. People are not as proud of their cars as they used to be, and often don't look after them in the same way, seeing them more as a necessary commodity to get people from A to B, rather than their pride and joy. However, if you can build a carport in an attractive and cost-effective way, it will add value to your property.

Sometimes you'll find that the property next door is in a terrible condition, for example, it needs painting on the outside, but the current owners won't do it. While it may sound crazy, you could offer to paint the front of their house, in order to make yours look more saleable! It won't be the first time a property developer has done this – I've even had to do this myself. The neighbours are normally delighted that you're going to do it for them, and it helps you sell your property faster, for little extra cost.

However, you might come up against next-door neighbour problems that are more substantial; for example, if you purchase a property next door to a hoarder. I once bought a house next to someone who wouldn't get rid of anything they possessed, including rubbish in their front and back garden! This is potentially a very serious problem, as it is usually extremely difficult to deal with such people, so I advise you to leave this problem for someone else. – don't buy that property.

This also applies to anybody who has cars jacked up on bricks in front of their house, or anything similar that is going to be detrimental to you selling your property. You can't guarantee being able to control or change the situation, so it's better not to purchase these properties. Ultimately, you have to be in control of your own destiny.

Also, remember that the outside of the house is important, including the back garden, so don't spend all of your money on the house itself, only to find you don't have enough funds to tidy the garden. Make sure the fence is in good repair and high enough to provide privacy from neighbours. Six feet is the maximum height you're allowed to put up by law in the UK, so if your neighbour is less than desirable, it's a good idea to utilise this full height.

You might be able to purchase more land from your next-door neighbour, or a property behind, and this would certainly increase the value of your house. This is called a 'marriage value', but please don't get carried away and spend £30,000 buying a postage stamp of extra garden! Check with your agent first, ensuring that it will add extra value and not result in you simply getting your money back, or even losing money.

Attics are another space that everybody gets very excited about. Firstly, you need to check the head height of the roof. If you think you could make a genuine room out of it and it wouldn't cost too much to convert, then it could be possible to add an extra room, such as a bedroom, or office. Still check with the agent, though, because the cost of doing so might be more than you could make back in that particular area.

When viewing a house with a cellar, be aware that they are very expensive to bring into domestic use, even if they have windows and it looks possible to make them into an extra room. It is both difficult and very expensive to make cellars habitable. My advice is to leave them alone, allowing interested buyers to think there is more potential in the house; hopefully they will think you have missed a trick by not developing the space yourself.

Remember, while some of these problems can help you to buy property for cheaper prices, they should also stop you from buying if you don't think you can get them under control and sort them out! It doesn't matter how cheap you can buy a property if you can't sell it. In such cases, it's not worth buying it in the first place.

So now you know how to get started, in the next chapter, we'll look at where and how to find property deals.

CHAPTER 2:
HOW TO FIND DEALS

Once you've decided what type of developer you are, and know a little about adding value, you'll want to start finding some deals. Its been said that, 'it's not what you know, it's *who* you know' and, in terms of finding property deals, this is certainly true. In this chapter, we'll look at the common places to find deals, including estate agents, deal finders, auctions and more.

Estate agents

Clearly, there are numerous ways of finding deals and the most obvious and old-fashioned way is by going to your local estate agent and asking what they've got on their books in the category you're interested in.

With estate agents, you need to build up a relationship if you want to forge a mutually beneficially partnership. This might mean popping your head around the door every couple of weeks, eventually buying the agent a coffee – and not forgetting the doughnuts! In this way, they remember you and what you are looking for. It also means they look forward to you coming in again. I have always written down in my notebook (more recently, on my mobile phone) anything memorable about my visit. It might be that the manager is about to have a baby, or someone is going on holiday. When I then go back two weeks later, I can start off the conversation asking how they got on, whether they had a nice holiday and so on. It's all about creating a connection and making it as easy as possible for them to like you and want to do business with you.

You need to be very clear with agents about *exactly* what type of property you want to buy and make sure they know it. If you're vague, they won't know whether to contact you or not. Bear in mind that when they've got a problem property, or an opportunity, they've probably got 50 other people they could ring. You have to make sure you're the first one on their list. If you can't answer the phone when they ring, make sure you get back to them straight away – don't delay! Definitely don't waste their time and don't mess them about, or next time you'll be the last one they call.

Deal finders

I often work with people who make a living off finding deals for developers such as myself. One deal finder I've worked closely with for 25 years. He often finds me deals, for which I pay him a finder's fee. I also pay him a fee when we sell the properties, even if he's not involved. This encourages the deal finder to pick up the phone to me first, before anyone else. If you not only pay the deal finder when they purchase the property, but when you sell it, they are far more likely to call you. I normally give the finder a 2% fee to find the deal for me and 1% when I sell. That's why I get offered the best deals! Deal finders will also help you to find buyers for properties you have purchased.

Your deal finder may well deal in property themselves and have their own portfolio of property. However, like everybody else, they can't buy everything, so if they find something that they can't afford to buy, they are normally very happy to pass it on for a fee. As you gain more contacts, this is something you can consider doing yourself. It's all about building up a network of people similar to yourself, where you all help each other.

Many years ago, we had a property consultant called Derek Hatton, who was the deputy leader of Liverpool City Council in the late 80s. Derek was his 'own man' and he wouldn't necessarily do what the Conservative Party wanted him to do, so they held back vital funding from Liverpool. He famously sent out redundancy letters to hundreds of Liverpool City employees by taxi, which brought the city to its knees. "It was meant to be a tactic – a way of buying time and meeting its legal obligation to stay within its budget," said Hatton at the time.

After he left the council, he set himself up as a property consultant and proved very useful to me at the time, as we were buying properties in and around Liverpool. We were paying him a monthly retainer – and we also had some great nights out! Paying a consultant on a monthly basis, like we did with Derek, is not something I would recommend early on in your property dealings, but it's certainly something you could consider later on, when you're consistently buying properties.

Property auctions

Property auctions are another great way of buying and selling property, more so over recent years. I am a director of Auction House UK, and since we bought the business in 2009, we've grown from seven franchises to 41, mainly due to the number of people who are looking to get into property investment. I have to say a big thank you to all the TV programmes, such as *Homes Under the Hammer*, that seem to be filming at one or another of our auctions around the country most weeks. It has been great free national advertising for us!

The great thing about buying and selling at auction is that it's **instant**. When the hammer comes down on a winning bid, the buyer has bought it and the seller has sold it, full stop. You then have 28 days to complete the sale. As part of my strategy, I always try to have a property for sale in every one of our auctions, as I know the money will then be coming in.

It's really important that you **always view a property prior to any auction**. Many years ago, I stuck my hand up on a lot in the Barnard Marcus auction in London, which was for a shop and three flats in Liverpool. I paid £15,000 for it and I thought I was very clever – until I viewed the property that is. Firstly, the tenant in the shop told me that he wasn't going to pay me any rent because he was looking after the shop and, if he hadn't been living there, it would have been boarded up – leading to it never being let, which was not a good start.

I then went to see the flat tenants, who basically told me the same; they didn't pay any rent because they were looking after the property and, if they were to leave, it would be vandalised! I came away from Liverpool feeling very deflated, as you can imagine. I then received a telephone call from my solicitor telling me that, in the small print of the auction contract, it stated that I had to pay all of the rent arrears to the owner and then attempt to claim it back myself from the current tenants.

At this point, I rang a friend of mine and asked him to drive up to Liverpool, replace a pane of glass in one of the flats that had been boarded up, repaint the front of the building within the day, and take photographs, all of which he did. I then put the lot back into the auction at the same reserve price and, thank goodness, I found a buyer who bought them at a similar price to what I paid. I was lucky, but you may not be – so always make sure you view the property prior to the auction.

Traditionally, you had to be very careful buying at auction, because there could be a good reason why a property was being sold that way; for instance, it could have subsidence, making it impossible to get a mortgage on the property. Auctioneers now have a legal responsibility to describe the property correctly in the catalogue. However, it is wise to check that the buildings next door and close by are not being used for a purpose that will be detrimental, preventing you from being able to sell the property on in the future.

With regard to the guide price stated in the catalogue, the reserve price should be between these two figures, so if the guide price is between £50,000 and £65,000, then the reserve price is likely to be £57,500. Always check with the auctioneer prior to the auction, to ensure that the guide prices have not changed. You can also ask them what the reserve price is, however, some may tell you, but some may not.

Just as with estate agents, it's a really good idea to get to know your local auctioneer. You'll find them very approachable. They are all great characters – a trait that's needed in order to be able to stand on the rostrum and do the job well. If you are thinking of bidding, introduce yourself before the auction starts and let them know that you will be bidding, **but do not tell the auctioneer what your maximum price is!** Not all auctioneers are as professional as Brian Baxter of Auction House UK, who auctioneers well over 100 times a year. Brian is one of the top auctioneers in the country, along with some of the auctioneers he has trained around the UK.

It's the speed of the auction process that I like, however, modern advances are making it more difficult to gain an advantage – such as all the legal packs now being online. It used to be the case that on the day of the auction, all of the hard copies of the legal packs were on a table. If you were interested in and bidding on a lot of properties, you could pick up the legal pack and not put it back until the auction was over – that way, no one else could read it. Although, sometimes they may announce in the room "Whoever has the legal pack for lot number XX, could they please hand it back".

Even now, you'll be surprised by how many people go to an auction and haven't read the legal pack beforehand, which means any future problems they may incur is their own fault, as far as I'm concerned. Fail to plan, plan to fail – it's as simple as that.

Don't get ruffled if they tell you that the legal pack has been downloaded 50 times and don't get excited if it's only been downloaded by two people before the auction either. I've kicked myself many times at an auction when I think a property is going to be very popular, so I haven't bothered to view it, only to find out that, in the end, it sells for a lot less money in the room than I thought it would.

Make sure that your solicitor has been through the legal pack prior to the auction and also that you have viewed it yourself. You'll be amazed at how many people do what is called 'bidding blind' – having not previously viewed the property, but still bidding because they thought it was cheap on the day. Most, however, have lived to regret it.

When I'm bidding at auction, I always set myself a limit and go no more than 5% over it. That way, if I've only missed it by a small amount, I'm not kicking myself because I know I've already gone 5% more than I should have. The trick is to set your limit and stick to it, plus 5% – don't get carried away.

Advertising

Another option is to put an advert in the local paper saying, 'Property bought for cash'. In tough times, you'll be taken back by how many calls you'll get! In the last recession, I did a modern spin on that and had a website built called Properties for Cash, which' for a while' was quite successful.

I find there is very little point these days in using paper advertising to sell your property, because everything is online; however, when it comes to finding properties, I've always had some success by putting small adverts in the local newspapers saying that I buy property for cash. You'd be amazed at how many older people ring up because they still read the paper.

Three years ago, I got a phone call on Boxing Day and didn't really want to answer, but I did. A chap said he'd seen my advert in the local Norfolk paper and wondered whether I'd be interested in buying his flat, to which I said, "Probably not". He said, "You don't even know how much I want for it yet." I said, "Well, you better tell me how much you want then!" He said, "I want £20,000, but I need it completed within two weeks". I looked at it in the first week of January and purchased it by the end of that week. In March that same year, I put it into my auction room in Norwich and sold it for £60,000. Thank goodness I picked up the phone!

Online

If you are computer literate and network on the Internet via LinkedIn, Facebook, and other social media channels, you should use them to your advantage by enquiring what's out there. It's really a case of nothing ventured, nothing gained. All these new sources are things that until now have been unavailable as part of the property developer's sourcing armoury.

I bought a property the modern way recently – off Gumtree. I paid 45k for it and, two months later, I popped it in to our next Auction House auction in Norwich and sold it for 78k without doing anything to it. I have to say though, that doesn't happen very often these days.

Planning portals

Another modern way to find out about properties is via the planning portal of each local authority. Everything is now in the public domain, with the address of the property and all of its drawings shown. Normally, details of the owner or agent dealing with the matter are also listed too, so it's a brilliant resource to find out who they are. You can then easily contact them and see whether they want to do a deal.

Associations and clubs

Another great source of contacts is being a member of an investment club, as you become privy to buy-to-let investments and other initiatives. Some of the property people who run these clubs buy houses or flats in bulk, at a large discount, and so are able to pass a discount on to you.

However, they do work on different systems. Some don't buy any of the properties, just working on commission with the developer, while others initially buy the properties in bulk themselves. If you are looking to do this, you need to check the actual selling prices of the flats or houses on the open market first. Don't just believe what the investment club says!

Landlord associations are also a great way of networking and meeting like-minded people. They normally know the up-to-date laws you need to be aware of, and can also recommend tradesmen who are tried and tested by other members.

Knocking on doors!

It might sound extremely old-fashioned, but if you see a vacant house, or one in poor condition, there is nothing wrong with finding out who owns it and seeing whether they wish to sell. Always start off with the neighbours, as they normally tell you everything you need to know, without even realising they are giving you the information you want. If not, visit the land registry website and, for very little money, you can do a search on the property and find out who owns it.

Knowledge is power, so if you can find out that the owner is short of money, or the property has been left to someone who lives abroad, offer them a deal. The fact that it's not being occupied and will deteriorate the longer it is left empty, should give them the incentive to deal.

One final tip on where to find deals comes from way back when I was training to be a racehorse trainer. Toby Balding, a very famous trainer who trained the Queen's horses, came to speak to us. His advice was very interesting – he said: "Never turn down a dinner party as you never know who you might meet." It's good advice as, while you might find a potential new racehorse owner, you might even find a financial backer, or a property deal!

CHAPTER 3:
PUTTING A DEAL TOGETHER

People outside the world of property development often think that you're just lucky and deals fall into your lap! However, this is not the case. Putting a deal together correctly takes time, effort and, in many cases, experience. In this chapter, I hope to help you save time and give you the expertise required to get the deal done properly.

So many potential deals fall by the wayside after a few weeks because of the seller's over-expectation, as they often haven't been given the right information and the deal hasn't been put together correctly. To avoid this, I always try to put together my deals by thinking one step ahead, anticipating any issues and problems that might arise during the purchasing process. To assist you with doing just that, I'll show you a simple step-by-step process for your first deal.

In this example, I'm assuming that you require a mortgage to purchase the property, that it's a pretty standard house in need of refurbishment, and that you are purchasing it via an estate agent. The basis of any purchase is the same, so hopefully this will help with any future purchases you make. We'll look more in depth at these topics in later chapters.

Finding your people

'Fail to plan, plan to fail'. In other words, get completely organised before you make an offer on the property. Don't make an offer and then run around excitedly trying to find the people you need – get your team in place before you start the process. People you will need to meet with prior to making any offer on a property are as follows:

- A mortgage broker – to find out how much you will be able to borrow.
- A solicitor or licensed conveyancer who is full time, appears to be on the ball, who you like – and who isn't about to go on a long holiday!
- A builder who understands what you want to do – make sure that you have spoken to someone else who has used them before.

When you've struck up a relationship with an agent, you can ask them to recommend these people, as it's a step in the right direction. There are also other ways to find the right people, such as through word-of-mouth and landlord associations. In chapters 10 and 11, I'll explain more about how to choose builders, estate agents, and solicitors.

Before making an offer

Depending on the condition of the property, ask your builder's opinion prior to making an offer. Write down exactly what you want done and they'll add to that list based on their experience.

Make sure you have asked at least two agents what they think the property will be worth once you have refurbished it. Explain to them the quality of the refurbishment you're going to undertake – and ask them both to put their valuation in an email to you. In my experience, what they say verbally and what they write down in an email can be very different. There's nothing like asking someone to put it in writing to concentrate their mind and help them come up with a more sensible valuation.

Any agent will be delighted to do this for you free of charge. Of course, they expect to be reselling the property for you. The golden rule of property is to **always give the resell back to the agent who sold it to you.** That way, they will help ensure the sale goes through smoothly for you in the first place. However, you can also tell the second agent that if the first doesn't sell it in the first month or so, then you'll pass the opportunity over to them.

When the offer is accepted

When you're happy, then make the offer. In the next chapter, we'll look at how to negotiate a good deal. When your offer has been accepted, you'll no doubt be asked how quickly you can complete the purchase. Always say 28 days from receipt of contract. It's highly unlikely that it will be done this quickly, but it's what the buyer and the agent want to hear. It's far more likely that this is the start of a 12-week process, but don't worry about that.

During the process, you will be pushed, harassed, and put under increasing pressure to perform quicker. Stay strong, keep cool, and remain in control of the deal. There is likely to be a time when you can turn the tables and put them under pressure yourself, especially if they get desperate to exchange and you discover all is not what you have been told via your legal team.

The agent dealing with the sale will ask who your solicitors are, and they will probably want proof of funds that you can purchase, or confirmation from your mortgage broker that you can get a mortgage/funding on the property. After this, you'll receive confirmation of the purchase from the estate agent. Check it to ensure it's *exactly* what you agreed.

At this point, get in touch with your mortgage broker again and make an appointment as soon as possible. At this appointment, you'll start getting the application forms filled in and get the valuation fee paid, so the property can be valued by the bank/building society who is lending you money on the property. Of course, you can't purchase the property until it has been valued and you have received a mortgage offer from the bank/building society. The sooner this is done, the sooner you are in a stronger position to purchase.

When the contract is received

Hopefully, your solicitor/conveyancer will then receive a contract by email from the seller. This can take a few weeks, if the seller wasn't organised prior to the sale, or if their solicitor/conveyancer is slow. Always ask your solicitor to let you know when the contract has been received. When it has, see your solicitor and ask them to quickly run through the basics of the deal.

You need to ensure there's nothing in there that concerns you. Many people leave this far too late, when the solicitor has already done enormous amounts of work. If there is something basic that the seller has not informed the agent about, it's likely to be exposed in the initial contract you receive.

Getting the local search done

Your solicitor/conveyancer then needs to apply for a local search. This is done by the local authority in the area you are purchasing in. It informs you of things such as a new road being planned close by, or a new housing estate – which these days is more likely! It will also show up any other local issues that may detract from the value of your new purchase.

These days, a local search can cost a few hundred pounds. As a result, some suggest waiting until all the other legal matters are sorted out, before asking for the search to be done. This is just in case there are other legal issues that would stop you purchasing the property, so saving you the cost of the search. However, if you're serious about buying the property, I believe in always getting on with it as quickly as possible. A search can take up to three weeks to come back from the local authority, so if you want to stay in control of the deal, just get it done!

Getting your ducks in a row

Your solicitor/conveyancer will then send the seller's legal team questions and enquiries. If there's any other questions you wish to ask, you need to do so at your initial meeting with them, such as who owns the back fence, etc. Hopefully, you will receive your mortgage offer by the time their solicitor/conveyancer has replied to all the enquiries raised and by the time the local search has come back from the local authority.

By this time, if the property needs a lot of work done, you should have a fixed price back from the builder you wish to use. If it's a big job, you may want to go out to competitive tender – in other words, ask three builders to quote for the work, all on the same basis. This can be achieved by creating a schedule of works, which a building surveyor will undertake for you.

Your solicitor/conveyancer is then required to report all the legal findings to the bank/building society who is lending you the money. They have to be satisfied that they're lending their money on a property that can be resold legally without any issues. If it can't be, you don't want to purchase the property, unless it's something that can be easily put right. This is a pretty standard process and is nothing to be concerned about.

When your solicitor/conveyancer is happy, the building society/bank lending you the money is happy, you have agreed a build price to get the work done, and you have a written valuation from one or two estate agents of what the property will be worth when refurbished – then you are ready to **exchange contracts**.

Reducing the price

At this point or at any point during the process, you can decide that you're paying too much for the property and look to re-negotiate on the price – especially if you have found something out that you didn't know when you originally agreed to purchase. I shall leave that decision up to your conscience and business acumen, but if you're going to try to reduce the price, only do so once you've sent the 10% deposit.

You can either ask your solicitor/conveyancer to inform the seller's side that you wish to reduce the price, or you can do it through the agent, who is used to dealing with this situation – even if they sound surprised and say they're not! If you're going to do this, **do not** inform the agent that you're just trying it on –even if you are and you're happy paying the full money anyway. Make sure they believe what you're saying.

Exchanging

There is a saying in property: 'exchange is the name of the game'. Of course it is, because once you have exchanged contracts, you are then the legal owner of the property! Your solicitor/

conveyancer will exchange contracts for you on your instruction. The completion date is set at this time, and it's normally 28 days. However, you can do it sooner or later as long as you can agree it with the seller. If you have any problems agreeing this, a good agent will deal with this for you.

Congratulations – the real work starts now!

Example deal...

Always make sure you write down your potential deal once you have viewed the property. It may well look different on paper than it does in your head!

Purchase price: £150,000

Solicitor's fees: £1,750 (plus VAT)
(Including all disbursements, such as search fees, money transfers and so on)

Stamp duty: £4,500
(3% of purchase price, paid via your solicitor)

Mortgage broker's fees: £1,600
(plus VAT) including valuation fee and so on

Agent's Finder's Fee: £3,000
(Plus VAT) If applicable 2% of purchase price, if they have found it for you and are not selling the property

Total purchase price: £162,120
Including VAT (which in normal circumstances is not recoverable)

CHAPTER 4:
NEGOTIATING TO BUY

Now you know how the process of putting a deal together works, the next issue is how to negotiate a good deal. It's said that a good outcome to any negotiation is one where both parties are happy. I'm not sure I actually agree with this, as I much prefer to be the happier! In this chapter, we'll look at how to successfully negotiate when buying and I'll give you some tips from my experience. Again, we'll assume that you're buying a pretty straightforward house for renovation. In the next chapter, we'll look at how to sell.

Making an offer

As I mentioned in the previous chapter, when you first make an offer on a property, keep your cards close to your chest. Don't let the right hand know what the left hand is doing.

If the agent asks you what your highest price is, tell them it's the offer that you've already made. You'll be amazed at how many people answer with the highest amount that they will go to. This makes the agent's job incredibly easy and, more importantly, won't get you a good deal.

Equally, never alienate the agent by offering such a low amount that it's insulting to them. Unless you have prior knowledge that there is a chance the offer will be successful, all it will do is annoy the agent and get their back up. Then, when you eventually come to a sensible offer, they may not take it out of principle. **You always need to make sure the agent is on your side** because, whether they get a few thousand more for the property or not makes virtually no difference to their commission, but it makes a huge difference to your profit margin.

I always try to find out the very bottom price the seller would accept as a sale from the agent, before I commit to any offer. It could actually be less than I was going to offer in the first place. Always let the seller commit themselves first.

Try to meet the seller

If it's possible, I always try to meet the actual seller of the property personally, rather than just going through the agent. This way, I can build up a rapport with the seller and find out more about them, why they're selling, and more about the property. This really helps if you want to tailor the purchase to a particular time frame. You'd be surprised at how many times a seller has said to me that it's not just about the money – it's about having an easy transaction without any hassle or worry, and one that is speedily concluded.

When you view the property, the owner often meets you these days, rather than the agent. In the past, estate agents would take you around every house, but now they don't tend to unless it's vacant. This is a great opportunity for you to get on well with the vendor, find out what they are likely to take, and see what their personal circumstances are. They also have far more knowledge about the property and what has or hasn't been done to it than the agent.

If you can meet the seller directly, try to connect with them within the first 10 seconds of doing so. It might be that you both have a dog or a cat, or when you walk in, you see a photograph of their daughter in university robes and your child is also at university. Whatever it is, find it quickly and start a connection with them.

If the owner doesn't show you around the property the first time, because the agent is doing this for them, then you can always ask to view the property again and ask to meet the seller. You have nothing to lose, because the worst they can say is no.

Using the information

When I meet the seller, I try to find out their situation, as **knowledge is power**. When you have the information, you can use it to your advantage. Most people will be doing the same in your situation, so there's nothing to feel embarrassed about. It doesn't mean you need to be aggressive and unhelpful, or unkind; in fact, the more helpful and kind you can be and the more rapport you get with the seller, the better.

A deal can be made easier for the seller, if you know what they wish to achieve from the sale and how quickly they want to sell. It may be that they don't want to clear out the house, because of all the memories there, or because they physically can't do so. In this case, I always say I will clear the property for them.

It may be that they need the money quickly and I am often able to help them do that. I've often bought property off people who, for one reason or another, are desperate to sell. For a lot of people, the amount is not the most important thing. Quality of life, peace of mind, and being able to move on quickly are often more important to them. For some people, money isn't everything.

When sellers are looking for a quick sale, if you've got cash to purchase the property (i.e. available funds, without any mortgage or borrowings), then one of the easiest ways to get the property at the right price is to offer a very quick exchange and completion. To do this, you need a solicitor who will work with you to make it happen fast.

However, sometimes the person selling the property wants flexibility, such as a quick exchange and a long completion to find an alternative property. This is something that you could work on with the seller, in order to secure the best deal. They may be prepared to exchange contracts with you and allow you into the property to do the building work before completion. This can be a very useful way of speeding up time between your purchase and resale and, obviously, anything that does this reduces the interest costs on your money as you can sell the property faster.

Basically, you need to make the deal as easy as possible for the owner, to ensure they sell it to you and no one else.

Reducing the price

If you need to reduce the price, it's better if you've met the seller directly and formed a good relationship. If you've already made a good impression on the seller and created respect, they are far more likely to work with you to sort any problems out. It could be that you need to reduce the price because something has come up on the legal side. It could be that you got overexcited and offered a little too much and now need to reduce the price in order for you to make at least 20% from the deal. It could be that you're just greedy and, at the last-minute, bid the price down on the day of exchange. This tactic can work depending on individual circumstances.

If you're going to try to reduce the price, make sure that the 10% deposit you are exchanging with has already been sent to the owner's solicitors, so they know you mean business. You'll be amazed sometimes at the response! I've had it done to me on numerous occasions, especially from other dealers. It's never nice, but it's business; sometimes it's for legitimate reasons, and other times it's not. In Chapter 14, we'll talk more about reducing the price.

Getting a delayed completion

Completion of the property transaction normally happens 28 days after exchange of contracts, and it can be reduced to almost immediately after the exchange. However, the completion date can also be extended further than 28 days, which is known as delayed completion.

If you have the opportunity to achieve a delayed completion on any purchase, it's normally good news. It can provide you with time to sell the property on for more money. If you wish to refurbish it, you might be able to get access to do building work on exchange of contracts. The sooner you can get a property back on the market, the better – as it's less time that you have your money out costing you interest. You might be asked for a larger deposit than normal to allow you access to the property, but it's still well worth doing.

Don't worry about what the seller is making

If you're buying a property that someone has only just bought themselves and are selling on to you quickly, never let the price *they* paid influence how much you will give them for it, should you find out this information. It doesn't matter how much profit they are making out of you. If you are confident that you can make the net profit you require yourself, then good luck to them.

Many years ago, in the early 90s, I purchased two large tower blocks of 280 flats in the West Midlands from an Irishman. He'd bought them six months earlier for £75,000 per block. I paid him £1.55 million knowing what he had paid. We still went on to make very good money out of them.

Success lies in being confident in your own ability and never worrying what profit someone else is making. In fact, quite often when I am selling something straight on to someone else, I tell them what I paid for it. That way, it's all out in the open and they can make their own decision.

With the internet and Land Registry, there's nothing you can't find out anymore, so being honest and to the point is the best policy. They are far more likely to pull out at a later stage if they find out the price you paid and you didn't declare it to them. I'd rather know straight away if there's a problem, than waste time with deals that fall through.

In the next chapter, we'll look at what happens when you come to sell the property.

CHAPTER 5:
HOW TO SELL PROPERTY

Once you've bought the property, you usually want to sell it on as quickly as possible, so you're paying as little interest as possible on the money you have borrowed, and so you can invest your profit into the next deal. In this chapter, we'll look at how to sell your property to get the best deal. Again, we'll assume that it's a standard house you have refurbished, though the principles are exactly the same whether you're selling one property, or five, or, as I have done, 150 at a time. Some of this is also relevant if you're planning to rent out your newly refurbished property.

Plan ahead

As with the process of purchasing, you need to do the same when selling – planning and being organised with your advisors! Do not leave anything whatsoever to chance. Always make it as easy as possible for yourself to sell the property. Don't make life any harder or stressful than it needs to be. Don't fall into the same trap that your seller probably did when you bought it i.e. not being organised with your solicitor/conveyancer well before the property goes on to the market.

Getting the sales pack ready

Ask your solicitor/conveyancer to organise a full legal sales pack, to send out immediately to the solicitor/conveyancer of the purchaser you are selling to – and double check that they have actually done it. You need to supply the following to your solicitor for the sales pack to be complete:

- Certificate relating to the boiler
- The electrical wiring certificate
- Any guarantees for the cooker and other appliances
- Guarantees for any timber treatment or damp treatment you've had done.

Make sure you have an up-to-date local search done and ready. One of my pet hates is that the local search is not carried out on the property until the mortgage offer has been received from the buyer. This drives me mad, because it slows down the sale. To counter this, I pay for a search on my own property. They last for three to six months. I can then pass it across to the buyer along with all the enquiry and property forms filled in, prior to the sale even being agreed. This way, as soon as you know who the buyer's solicitor is, you can send them a full pack of legal documents.

These queries are the ones that your solicitor/conveyancer asked the last time around, along with a few more. Don't take a 50/50 gamble on whether the solicitor/conveyancer for the other side of the sale will pick up on some small legal issue that you could have dealt with beforehand.

Make sure the guarantees are in place from the builder. I can tell you from experience, that there is nothing more frustrating than when you're asked for these things by the buyer's solicitor/ conveyancer and you can't find them, because the builder didn't supply them, or left them in the property and they have gone missing. Getting replacements is a nightmare, so don't go there! Getting this done in advance can save at least a month.

Putting the property on the market

When you have seen proof of a full sales pack ready to send out immediately via your solicitor/conveyancer, you can put the property on the market. **Do not** be tempted to put it on the market before it is finished, unless it's a large scheme and you have a show house/apartment for buyers to look around.

Putting the property on the market is an exciting time! I always compare it to the opening night of the theatre – you think you've got it right and everything is spot on, but it's the public who will ultimately tell you whether you have or not. It doesn't actually matter what you think!

Getting the property up to scratch

Because you'll have saved time getting your full legal pack organised in advance, you can use this time to get your property in first-class condition before being marketed. Once the builder has completed their work, go around the property without them and write down anything that still needs to be finished correctly in each room – called the **snagging list**. There will always be small things that aren't right – this is quite normal. I've never met a builder yet who gets it all right on the first snagging list – it always takes at least two attempts! When they say they've completed it, check the property again.

To encourage the builder to totally finish your property, make sure they still have some money to come at the end of the job.

This is normally called a retention fee, and it's approximately 5% of the value of the job. They normally get it after three or six months, although you can negotiate on that if you wish.

Organise a professional **builder's clean** at the end, once the builder has finally shut the front door. There is nothing more frustrating than having professional cleaners in, only to find out that the builder has to come back and will make more mess. Never get the builders to do the final clean as it will be a disaster!

Don't forget the externals, including the garden. Make sure that all building rubbish is gone and that the outside of the property is looking sharp. Ensure that the fences have been repainted, or are brand new, that the grass is cut, and there are no weeds anywhere. The property needs to **look better than any other property on the market at a similar price**, because that's how you're going to sell it before the others sell. We'll look more in-depth at this process in Chapter 8.

Choosing an agent

If you've refurbished a house, there is an unspoken agreement of 'honour amongst dealers/agents' that you sell it through the agent you bought it from. By now, I'm hoping you have an excellent relationship with your agent and they are already looking for the next deal for you. They will be more encouraged to sell this one quickly, if they think you're going to buy another one from them.

If you have no loyalty to an agent, because you didn't buy the house from an agent, the easiest way to find the best agent is on Right Move – see who has the most properties for sale. 'Success breeds success' is a true saying. The more they have for sale, the more they have sold. You'll never see a successful mid-range estate agent with no properties to sell.

Please don't get sucked in by online agencies where you pay

an upfront fee to sell your property. They have absolutely no incentive to sell it once you've paid them and absolutely every incentive to tell you it's worth more than it is – to persuade you to pay them their upfront fee. More often than not, you will still end up having to get a traditional estate agency to sell it for you. The only time, in my view, you will ever make any money selling on such sites is in a market where properties are in very short supply. I firmly believe that their business model is flawed. Even if they find you a buyer, they have no incentive to make sure the sale goes through successfully.

Also, never put the property on the market with more than one agent at a time. If you do, you will cheapen your product. The more agencies it's on with, the less the agents will try to sell it, and the more desperate you will look. You may think "The more competition, the more they will try to sell it for me", but this is not the case. You need your agent to be loyal to you, so they need to like you, respect you, and want to do their best for you.

Getting a valuation

When the property is ready and you've picked the agent, let them come round – and make sure they take their shoes off at the doorstep! Before they commit to giving you a price, tell them that you wish to have a sale agreed within six weeks. When the agent has looked at the property, they'll give you a valuation.

If the estate agent sold it to you in the first place and advised you what it would be worth once refurbished, it won't be a surprise when they tell you what they think they can sell it for.

Once they have given you the price, don't be tempted to ask for thousands of pounds more, as they are the experts – and this is how they make their living. You want to crack on and buy another property, not take gambles.

All estate agents are extremely optimistic in my experience. They have to be to do their job well, as they want to have your property on their books for sale, rather than on another agent's books, so they are likely to overvalue your property. They will then try to work the price down over the coming months to a figure where it sells. However, for a property dealer, this is completely the wrong way of doing it!

Setting the property sales price

Nearly everyone selling a house asks for it to be put on the market for more money than it's valued at, bearing in mind that the agent is going to stand on the optimistic side of what you can get. This is a mad idea!

What you *should* be doing is putting the property on the market at a **slightly lower figure than what the agent recommends**. To some people, this sounds crazy, but everything I put on the market I want to sell within 28 days, so I can move on to the next deal quicker. I'm not kidding myself that, just because I own it, it's worth more. I accept that, now and again, property makes liars out of people; in other words, sometimes you can get more money for a property than it's actually worth, but we're not here to take gambles.

Any property has its biggest impact on the market within the **first two or three weeks** of being put up for sale. If it's overpriced and you don't get the response you want, which you won't, you will have lost all impact by the time you reduce it to what it should have been. Everyone has already seen it and it's now stale on the market. Of course, this depends on the time of year, as the market is slower over holidays and Christmas, so also take the time of year into account.

If you get frustrated because the property is not selling, then by all means freshen it up by taking it off the market for two to three weeks, then putting it back on with a new agent at a further reduced price – you have to give the new agent the chance to sell it and, if it goes on at the same money as before, it's unlikely to have the same impact.

Agreeing the agent's fee

Now you need to agree the fee you're going to pay the agent for selling the property. You should be paying between 1% to 2% of the sales price. I never push the selling agent down to a very cheap fee. The reason for this is that I want them to do a really good job for me and sell my property before any others. I want to work with them in the long term as they could well be a source of some very good deals.

Remember that your agent needs to make a living and they are doing an incredibly important job for you, so you should pay them a decent commission for doing so. You want the job done well and professionally, so hitting them hard when negotiating the fee is false economy. You want your agent on your side, trying to get the most for you – not telling a potential buyer that you're desperate to sell and would take a big reduction.

If you sign a sole agency agreement with them, read the small print and ensure it doesn't say 'sole selling rights', because this means that if you bump into a friend who decides they want to buy your property, the agent can still come after you for their commission. If you do sell it privately, you might still like to pay the agent something anyway because, hopefully, they're going to find your next deal. However, it's nice to have that choice!

At this point, make sure that you like all the internal and external photographs the agent takes. If you can, always help the agent out by letting them put up a for sale sign. Make sure you receive the brochure as quickly as possible.

Ask them when the property will be going live on the website. Don't worry if they don't advertise in newspapers, as newspaper advertising is pretty much finished in terms of selling houses. It's all about online search sites, such as Right Move and Zoopla, or certain sites for specific properties, for example, equestrianproperty.co.uk.

Getting offers

When the agent calls you and says you have received an offer, never sound relieved or excited. The first thing to ask is **how much** will the buyer go to? If this happens, you need to play the game. Suggest they come back to you with their **best price**. Once you have that, you can then use that as the base price to negotiate from, so you've automatically increased the offer without committing.

This can save you a lot of time and effort before you commit to a decision. You don't have to give an answer to an offer immediately. It's prudent to thank them for it, ask the right questions, then think about it – but not for too long! You don't want the buyer to lose enthusiasm because you're taking too long to decide.

If you start getting offers within the first day or two, you can always say "Thank you for your offer, I'm just waiting to see how many more offers we get in the first week". If you have two or more people who want it at the asking price, get the agent to ask buyers for their very **best and final offer on a certain day and time.**

Choosing the buyer

Contrary to what you might think, the highest offer may not be the best one to take! Don't necessarily pick the buyer offering the most – always pick the **best buyer**. You need to make sure the buyer can proceed quickly, because every day that goes by will cost you money in interest charges and will rob you of the opportunity to buy another deal. If you have the opportunity to meet the buyer, do so. If there's more than one, see which one you get on with best and feel you can trust the most.

Make sure your agent has checked a potential buyer's financial position and ability to purchase, ensuring that they can either get a mortgage, or prove cash funds. The best buyer is often a cash buyer, but make sure they are very motivated to purchase. Ask the agent to check them out and make sure they're not offering on numerous other properties at the same time, or have a reputation for not proceeding.

I'm always very suspicious of buyers who want to buy the property immediately after viewing it. In my experience, they normally pull out. Likewise, if someone comes around to view for the third time, they don't normally buy – as they're too busy looking for reasons why they shouldn't!

If the buyer making the offer is in a chain of sales, get the agent to check that the chain is complete and that everyone is able to proceed. If there is a chain behind your buyer, it is vital that the agent investigates the chain thoroughly, to make sure everyone is in a position to move forward. Otherwise, this can cause big problems down the line.

If you have a choice between buyers and one buyer is **not** in a chain, my advice is normally to take their offer – even if it's for a lower amount. It will be a much simpler transaction and you will be in control all the way through. When your agent is dealing with a number of other properties being sold, it can become very complicated. The more sales, the higher the risk of one of them falling through.

Negotiating the price

Where there is a difference between the asking price and the offer, I often use the tactic of splitting the difference. Once I think I'm getting close to their maximum figure, it squeezes a little bit more out of the deal for me. Then, should there be any issue before exchange of contracts where I need to reduce the price slightly, it will hopefully only be the extra that I managed to squeeze out of them, so I'm happy to accept that.

If you get a really low offer, then the buyer is probably taking liberties. There are buyers out there like that, who think they are being clever. You should stand up to them. Be polite, decline the offer, but try to keep talking to them. If it's their only offer and you refuse it, you can take some comfort from the fact that they were probably never going to buy it in the first place. Just as if they view it for the third time, it's unlikely they will proceed.

Always take the advice of your agent, as that's what you're paying them for. They will be less biased than you and are not as close to the situation as you are, so they can make a more rational decision. Never make a decision about an offer on the basis that you are cross about the amount! In the cold light of day, it might be your best offer in the short to medium term. That's the call you have to make, considering all of the circumstances.

Always be thinking about the next deal. Hopefully you've already got in mind what you are going to buy next, so be practical and don't be greedy. If you're making a good profit, accept a compromise and get on with it.

Progressing the sale

Getting a buyer is really just the start of the agent's job, not the end – as 25% of buyers do not proceed to completion. Many agents have a dedicated sales progression team, whose job it is to look after the sale on your behalf through to completion. The purchaser needs to choose the right solicitor too, as it can make a huge difference to the sales process. Quite often, the selling agent will recommend a good solicitor/conveyancer to the buyer, one who they have successfully worked with before. This will help to ensure a smooth transaction.

Similar to the process of purchasing a property, the two sets of solicitors/conveyancers then exchange information. The buyer gets their mortgage offer through and they are then in a position to exchange, but you must continue to drive the sale forward via your solicitor/conveyancer, too. When you first meet them, explain that you expect to receive responses within a few hours when chasing up sales or purchases. If they can't respond that quickly, my advice is to find one that will.

Make sure your solicitor responds immediately to any queries the buyer raises. Ask the agent to check the sale every seven days and report back to you. Also ask them to tell you when the mortgage valuation is being done or, if it has been done, when the buyer's mortgage offer will be sent out. Make sure the buyer is still motivated and working to the correct timescale. If the agent is good, they probably have their mortgage broker arranging the mortgage for the buyer, which is a great help, because you can find out what's going on at any time.

If the buyer is in a sales chain, this may include three or even four properties. These properties also have to be sold down the line and **completed on the same day as yours** in order for yours to sell. So, you need to ensure the agent checks that everybody in the chain of properties is in a position to crack on and complete their purchases quickly.

As you are super-organised and have your legal pack ready to be sent out, you can tell the buyer that they have 21 days to exchange contracts, after which you can tell them you may wish to put it back on the market. I always put my buyers on a 21-day exchange from receipt of the contract sent from my solicitor. As with anything, we all know it probably won't happen in 21 days, but at least if you set a target, it might happen just a week, not months later!

The timescale makes both the buyer and their solicitor/ conveyancer concentrate and realise that we mean business. It normally concentrates the mind and gets them to proceed quickly. Of course, in reality, it may not happen within that timescale, but you are then in the driving seat all the way through the transaction, which is where you need to be.

Overcoming problems

Even when you're super organised, things can still go wrong. By following the previous tips, you are reducing the risk dramatically. However, quite often you have to accept the fact that your sale is part of a chain and they all need to complete on the same day. Clearly, the longer the chain, the higher the risk of the sale falling through, as somewhere down the chain, one of the people might pull out of their purchase.

In a chain of sales, a common problem is when one of the properties in the chain is downvalued. This means the sale has been agreed, but the property is valued by a qualified surveyor at less than the agreed price, normally for mortgage purposes.

The buyer of that property can't proceed – and you have an incomplete chain, so the buyer of your property can no longer proceed either. None of the properties can be sold unless the owners of the property will accept the reduced price. In most cases, the buyer is not financially able to do that. There is nothing more frustrating than your buyer having a problem because three houses down the line in the chain there's a problem.

However, you can stay in control here. If everyone in the chain agrees to reduce their sales price slightly, it can add up to the **total amount of the downvaluation** on the problem property. So, if this problem occurs, ask your agent to get hold of every other buyer's agent in the chain. Each agent needs to speak to their clients and explain that if everyone reduces their agreed selling price by a small amount, it will make up the difference on the property that has been downvalued – so everyone can still proceed. This way, everyone still gets to move and any loss is shared across all the properties in the chain, including yours.

Once I have a buyer, I will do anything and everything to make sure I get the sale through. I have no pride when it comes to getting a sale through to completion. If you have, you are more likely to cause the sale to fail when there's a problem. Accept it with a smile on your face – that's my best advice (within reason)!

Being asked to reduce the price

It never ceases to amaze me how many times I am asked to reduce the price close to exchange of contracts, for one reason or another – from school teachers to vicars and everyone else in between. Often, it's because the survey hasn't come out quite as well as the buyer would have hoped, or because the property is downvalued. It could be that the buyer is just being difficult, thinking they've got the upper hand, which in some cases they do, especially if they need the money for another purchase.

In my experience, the buyer will normally ask for double the amount than they will actually accept. The better you got on with the buyer, the less likely they are to try this on. They will be embarrassed to do so if they feel they know you personally. Also, if the agent has some gumption, they should head off any problems like this before they gain traction. However, most people will still try it on if they're brave enough.

It's never nice when this happens, but if it does, stay calm and cool. Keep smiling and speak to your agent to find out whether the buyer is just trying it on, or whether they genuinely have a problem. Make your judgement, a lot of which will depend on whether you've got your eye on another property to buy – where you can make even more money. Of course, it will also depend on the market conditions at the time.

On the whole, I usually agree to some renegotiation. Having gone that far down the line, the prospect of having to start a sale all over again is not desirable, considering the risk that you might get less the second time around. Every extra day it takes to sell your property is another day of interest you're paying. In addition, you can't move on to the next deal quickly.

Don't be afraid to question yourself, and the most obvious question is: "Do I want the money in my bank account as soon as possible?" The next question is: "Am I willing to be as flexible as possible to make sure it happens?" The answer, of course, should always be **yes**! Unfortunately, some people let other issues get in the way, so make sure you have a clear vision of your end goal. Remember, pride comes before a fall!

If it doesn't sell

Over the years, I have had so many people ask me why their house hasn't sold. I ask them all the same question: "How long has it been on the market?" They might say six months, nine months, or a year. My answer to them is always the same. Every property in the UK sells if it's priced right, whatever it is.

You may be able to make it a lot *easier* to sell, but they all sell at the right money. I've heard every excuse under the sun why their house hasn't sold, but the hard fact is that, if it's priced right, it will sell. If we haven't sold a property that we have on the market after a month then, unless there is a high level of interest in it, I reduce the price.

However, this does depend on the time of year, as the market is slower during holidays and the Christmas period, where I might reduce it after six to 10 weeks instead. As such, there's usually less interest in December, January, and August – whereas there is more interest in April, May, June, and July. When it comes to selling, different months affect the sales timescales.

There is no point in kidding yourself about the price. It doesn't matter in the end what you think it's worth, or what the agent thinks it's worth, as the only thing that matters is the person who will make an offer on it.

Completing the sale

Hopefully, nothing will go wrong and they won't try to reduce the price at the last minute. If they try to change the completion date, don't worry too much, as the most important thing is to exchange. If they need an extra two weeks to complete, just make sure they pay the full 10% deposit.

Most solicitors like at least a week in between exchange and completion, so they can get the funds in from the lenders and work out what the balance is. They also may have documents that need signing – normally between exchange and completion. However, it is possible to do it immediately, and sometimes this can be very helpful.

It's always a great feeling when you have exchanged contracts and made money from the property deal. Of course, it's soon forgotten as you will be on to the next one. Remember, you're only as good as your next deal!

Example of sales costs...

The following costs, assuming sale is completed after
nine months of ownership

Total builder costs: £38,545 (inc VAT)

Interest on loan: £6,037.50
(On an example where you borrowed £115,000
for nine months at 7%)

Carpets: £2,100 (plus VAT)

Empty council tax rates: £740

Electricity used: £210

Solicitor's fees: £850 (plus VAT)

Estate agent's fees: £3,675
(1.5% sale price plus VAT)

Total refurbishment costs: £53,482.50
Plus the purchase price and associated costs: £162,120

Total costs: £215,602.50
LESS property sales price of £260,000

Result is a total net profit after all costs of £44,397.50
Which is a net profit of 21%

CHAPTER 6:
FUNDING DEALS

There are a number of ways to fund property deals. For the very lucky, with large cash funds available, this chapter doesn't really apply, however, for most people in the real world, funds are normally tight or non-existent. There are numerous options open to you, and I honestly believe that if the deal is good enough, then somebody will put up the money for you.

Financial backers

A financial backer is someone who is prepared to offer you a certain amount of money in order for you to purchase a property – on the understanding that they will get their money back first and then share any profits with you 50/50, or, in some cases, get more of a share than you. You are putting in your time and expertise; they are taking the risk on the deal.

Over the years, I've been guilty of using my financial backers too much; not doing enough deals independently on my own. However, the problem is that, if you don't feed your financial backer with deals, they will go and find someone else to do deals with. It's a real advantage to have someone with financial clout behind you, as proving you have the funds when you purchase is clearly a lot easier. They also deal with all the financial aspects of the transaction, leaving you to concentrate on what you're good at – doing the deals.

Most backers I deal with give me 33% to 50% of the net profit, but I make sure I take no costs out of the transaction until the deal is totally complete and the proceeds are shared out. If you start wanting to take money out for expenses along the way, you are in danger of losing your backer's confidence in you. You need to be seen as financially secure and genuine, not in need of handouts as the project proceeds.

It's imperative that you quickly get the confidence of your backer. Always under-promise and over-deliver. That way, when you say it's worth £300,000 and you sell it for £310,000, they will have complete and utter confidence in you for the next deal.

Most backers will test you with a small deal first, which is very sensible. As you get to know each other, they will then lend you more as their confidence in you grows. With any new backer, I always suggest starting off with a very small deal that you definitely know you can over-deliver on. You will quickly gain their trust, confidence, and respect for doing so.

Remember, if all goes well and you get on with them, it may result in you making a lot of money together, so don't spoil it by being greedy on the first deal, or subsequent deals for that matter.

I have personally worked with some backers for 35 years and I have never fallen out with any of them. Even if you're not putting any money up, it's important that you offer to guarantee any loss there might be if the transaction goes wrong, on the same basis as your share of the profit.

Bank funding

For those who like to be in charge, the main banks are still an option, but, realistically, only if you're looking to borrow 50% of the purchase price, or less. Currently, they like to ask you what your track record is with deals, so if you haven't done a deal before, they may not lend you the money.

You also need to understand the bank's rates and fees. When they tell you, for example, that they will lend you the money at 5% over base, there will also be costs for borrowing the money in the first place. These costs are traditionally 1% to 2% of the amount of the loan, and the same when you complete the sale and pay it all back. It all adds up, so know what you're in for, down to the last pound.

Depending on who you're dealing with, it can also take up to three months for a bank transaction to actually produce the money. Once they've had your inside leg measurement and know every monthly expense you have, probably including how much you spend on haircuts, they will ask you to pay for the valuation. This will be undertaken by a chartered surveyor, but not on your behalf – on the bank's behalf!

If the valuation comes back favourably, they will then instruct their solicitors, which you yourself will be paying for on top of your own solicitor's costs, to deal with the legal funding side of the transaction.

They will also have a first charge on the property, meaning they legally get their money back first. This guarantees that they are repaid in full, before anyone else gets any proceeds from the sale. So, if you're buying three houses, you probably won't get any money back on the first two until they have been paid off. You could possibly negotiate that they only take 80% of the money on each sale, which they might do, so it's worth discussing this with them.

However, a word of caution. We did a similar deal on a block of 12 flats in Clacton-on-Sea during the recession. When we sold the first one, the bank took all the money. When we queried it and said we agreed 80%, they said "Yes, we did at the time, but now we want to call in all of the proceeds on each flat until the loan is repaid". So, they can always change their minds too.

Specialist property banks

Since the 2008/9 recession, a number of specialist property banks have emerged. They started up in competition with the big banks, which took a financial hammering during the recession, so have not been particularly enthusiastic about lending on property since. These new banks are much easier to deal with and lend you the money more quickly. They normally lend up to a maximum of 70% to 75% loan to value. This means that if the property value is £100,000, they will lend between £70,000 and £75,000.

I use these banks a lot, as they normally get the transaction concluded within 28 days and they are used to dealing with issues and problems in property deals. They increase the choice and competitiveness of the market, making much quicker decisions than traditional banks. However, they are looking to make healthy profit, so the interest rates they charge may be more

Bridging finance loans

Bridging loans are normally used for short-term lending of anything up to 12 months and can be repaid at any time during that period. Traditionally, it is more expensive to borrow money from them than normal banks, however, they also move much quicker. They are used to dealing with auction buyers who need quick decisions. You can usually get the money within 14 days of applying for it, which can be very useful in certain circumstances; for instance, if you're buying at auction and you don't have time to go through the formal applications at a regular bank.

However, this sort of lending is not for the faint-hearted, or non-risk-takers. Bridging finance companies normally lend up to 80% of the purchase price, and charge anything from 8% to 15%. They will also take on people who may not have a good credit history. Of course, the bigger the risk to them, the more they will charge you in interest.

They also don't normally want to lend for more than 12 months at a time, so you need to make sure you can definitely repay the loan in that time. Compared to other lenders, they are ruthless. I'm certainly not against using bridging finance to purchase a property. Just remember that the interest will be a lot higher, so pay the money back as soon as possible. Otherwise, you'll make a lot less profit.

Personal guarantees

These days, what you must remember is that all banks are likely to want you to sign a personal guarantee for the amount of the loan you are borrowing. This is a subject very close to most people's hearts. Of course, in an ideal world, you would never sign a personal guarantee to a bank, but that's the way it is.

Before the last recession, I was very proud of the fact that I had no personal guarantees for any of my borrowing. However, that soon changed when the property recession arrived. The banks then forced me to give personal guarantees on our current borrowing, which of course I did my very best to argue against.

It's now virtually impossible to borrow money without giving some form of personal guarantee, even if it's not for the whole amount you are borrowing. My advice, therefore, is to grin and bear it. If you have a husband, wife, or life partner, make sure they are aware of this and that the bank doesn't insist on getting a guarantee from them too.

If you're borrowing the money in your own name, you are automatically personally guaranteeing the bank loan, because you are the person borrowing the money. If you are the director of a limited company and are borrowing via the company, the bank will almost certainly ask **you** to sign a personal guarantee on behalf of your limited company. This is normally for the full amount you are borrowing. This means that if the limited company can't pay the money back because there is a problem, then they will come to you personally to get it paid off.

If you get yourself in a muddle with a loan and the bank asks you to repay it, never bury your head in the sand. Always respond to them, sit down with them, and negotiate a payment programme over a period of time that suits you and that you can repay. At the end of the day, most banks will prefer to help and be flexible in their approach rather than ending up having to take you to court, so use that to your advantage. Never, ever fall out with the bank.

What I would say about borrowing money from banks is that, even if the interest rate is very high, it's still a lot cheaper than giving away between 50 and 80% of your profit with a financial backer, so this is something you need to personally weigh up.

Building societies

We are incredibly fortunate in this country to have building societies, which were originally non-profit-making organisations set up to lend on houses for people to live in, rather than as an investment. Most building societies have now been converted into banks, but they are still unique to the UK, not operating in any other country in the world. This is one reason why property in the UK is so easy to borrow money against, compared to the rest of the world.

One way of financing a property deal is to borrow money from a building society and live in the property for a short period of time before selling it on. I've known a number of house owners to repeat this over the years and make a career of it.

Buy-to-let mortgages

The buy-to-let market has really exploded over the last 20 years. In the past, it was only people like me – professional property investors, – who used traditional banks to buy properties to rent out. With the introduction of buy-to-let mortgages, this sector of the market is open to many more people at much higher levels of borrowing than was previously available.

Buy-to-let lenders assess your affordability, not only on your personal circumstances, but also take rental value into account as well as the value of the property and the current market. For instance, if the property is rented at £750 per month and the mortgage is £500 per month, then I would consider this affordable and I would believe many lenders would too. The maximum loan-to-value ratio (the amount of the mortgage against the value of the property) is usually 75%.

However, be aware that you need to consider all costs, such as general repairs, insurance, rent voids (periods where the property is vacant, or the tenant is not paying), and the tax that is payable on rental income.

Despite the costs, some people, to their great credit, have managed to build up very large residential portfolios. While property values are increasing, you can quickly build a large portfolio this way. Most buy-to-let mortgages come with a fixed interest rate for the first two years. Your mortgage advisor will no doubt contact you towards the end of those two years to see what other rates are available. Not only might it be worth moving lenders, but if you have improved the property and the property market has increased during that period of time, it may be worth seeing whether you can borrow more money on the property because it's gone up in value. This way, you can get a deposit together for another purchase.

This is all very well, until the market drops. In Chapter 13, we'll look at what to do when the property market drops. When you can see this happening, my advice is to sell some properties. Get them on the market straight away and don't hang out for the highest price possible. Other people may not realise the market is dropping as you do, but they soon will! Then reduce the loans you have on the ones you keep. Use the sales money to bring the loans down to 50% of the value of each property. This will make sure that they are very easily covered by any rent coming in on the properties.

Mortgage broker

If you can find a good mortgage broker, they are worth their weight in gold. They're hard-working, helpful, responsive, and know their market inside out. Most of the specialist property banks I mentioned earlier are only accessible via your mortgage broker and don't have a high street presence, so your mortgage broker becomes even more important.

Also bear in mind that the last thing a bank wants is to accommodate early redemption, i.e. when you wish to pay off a property loan earlier than you envisaged. If you take out a 25-year mortgage and want to pay it all off after 15 years, the bank will allow you to do so, but within the small print of the loan agreement, there will normally be a financial penalty for this. This is because they have to re-lend the money to someone else, so they penalise you for paying back a loan early. Before you take out the loan, make sure you know how much they are charging for early redemption should you wish to do so.

Mortgage brokers charge a fee for finding you the right mortgage and also receive a fee from the building society or bank. However, don't begrudge a fee from anybody who helps you – it's very short-sighted! If you can build up a good rapport with your mortgage broker, they almost become your funding partner, but at a much cheaper price.

A mortgage broker may also suggest a number of add-ons where they can earn extra commission, such as redundancy insurance. In your case, it may not be necessary, so be wary of them piling on things that you just don't need. It's similar to when you buy a TV or washing machine – they often ask whether you want to take out an extended warranty, which they end up making more money from than selling the actual product.

Private loans

When interest rates are desperately low, there are more people willing to lend you money privately. These are normally people you already know. They are usually receiving less than 1% interest at their bank or building society on their savings, so will be delighted to receive 6% to 10% interest per annum from you – as long as the risk is minimal and short-term.

As with financial backers, it's much better to start borrowing small amounts and build up their confidence in you, rather than trying to borrow too much straight away and frightening them off. They may not be commercially-minded, so my advice is to slowly gain their confidence. If you can find someone willing to give you a private loan, it's a much cheaper alternative than having a backer.

Family

This may, in fact, be your first port of call when trying to raise money to buy an investment property and, in many cases, it will be your best prospect. Always bear in mind that if you are borrowing from your parents and have brothers and sisters, they may not be impressed that your parents are lending you the money and not them.

Always treat an investing family member like any other investor and offer to pay the same rate of interest, share of the profits, or both. This way, it appears much fairer to any other family members. If it's successful, I'm sure the family member would lend you money again.

We all have to start somewhere, and I was very fortunate that my mother lent me a small amount of money on my 18th birthday, so I could buy my first two investment properties. I did pay her a rate of interest and gave her a share of the profit, which she was delighted to receive. Guess what, she lent me more money the second time to do the next deal! I will always be incredibly grateful to her, as she believed in me from a very young age.

Inheritance

If you are fortunate to have an inheritance coming to you in the future, it may be worth asking whether you could have it sooner. Explain that it will be more helpful for you to get on the investment ladder, undertaking a property deal now, than it would be in the future.

Depending on the size of the inheritance, there could be a saving of 40% inheritance tax if it's given to you now and if the person giving it lives for seven years. Please take legal and professional advice on this point, as rules and regulations may change fairly quickly.

I appreciate that it can be a very difficult conversation to have with your relatives, but if you're going to deal or invest in property, sometimes being forthright and asking honest questions can be the difference between doing a deal or not doing one. It could be the boost you need to make yourself a lot of money in the future, and the person bequeathing the inheritance might actually enjoy seeing you putting it to good use. So ask.

PART 2:
IN-DEPTH
PROPERTY INVESTING

CHAPTER 7:
WHAT TYPE OF PROPERTY TO BUY

I often get asked what's the best type of property to buy as a property developer? Houses or flats? In the town or the country? Residential or commercial? And what about new builds? In this chapter, I'll weigh up the pros and cons of the different types of property.

Town vs rural area

One of the questions you might have when choosing which property to buy is whether to buy in a town or a rural area? For me, the biggest consideration here is to always make it as easy as possible to sell. Why stack the odds against you? If you buy in a city or town, you've probably got thousands of people looking for property in that area. Depending on how expensive the property is, this should give you a certain amount of confidence. Even if the market isn't great and the amount of people looking has gone down from 1000 to 500, that's still a lot of people looking!

On the other hand, in the countryside, or in a small village, you're limited in the number of people who want to live in that area. This might only be 30 to 50. It also depends on how many bedrooms you've got, meaning you could be down to only one or two buyers looking.

You may say "Well, it's a really pretty village and it's always very popular." But let me tell you, I've bought in villages like that and all that glisters is not gold. They may be lovely places and people may wish to visit them on a regular basis, but it doesn't mean they want to spend the winter in the village, with no local shops or pub, or amenities that are under threat of closure. Not to mention the poorer internet connection there!

Of course, there are always exceptions to the rule. In some special small villages, people like to have a second home, so they will always have more buyers. However, finding those properties is difficult. For example, Southwold in Suffolk is so popular that anything that appears on the market – even if in need of dire restoration – goes for more than it should do, meaning there is very little possibility of making any profit. I purchased a few properties over the years there and I wish I'd kept them!

If you are tempted into villages, make sure the property is not thatched, as this can cause numerous problems. Not only does replacing the thatch on a detached house cost between £30,000 and £50,000, depending on whether you have straw or reed, but most thatchers get booked up for a couple of years in advance. Also, the extra risk of fire and higher insurance premiums put people off purchasing. I should know as I used to live in one!

So, my position on where to buy, is to **play it safe**, certainly initially. Go where the population is.

Residential vs commercial

When it comes to the question of residential or commercial properties, you can probably tell that I am biased towards residential property – on the basis that it is generally a much safer investment than commercial property. The number of shops in the UK has declined rapidly over the last thirty years. The reason for this is because more people own cars than in the past, so there's been a massive increase in out-of-town shopping at supermarkets and other outlets. This means that local shops are less likely to be required.

More recently, the internet has transformed shopping habits. At my home, the infamous white van turns up on a daily basis, coming up my drive at great speed to deliver one item that my wife or children have purchased! I haven't succumbed to this form of shopping yet, but no doubt it's only a matter of time. As the times change, so do investments. With less shops being required, it's not surprising that I believe residential to be a safer bet.

Even with secondary shop investments, in other words, shops that aren't on the main high street or close by, it's very difficult to get quality tenants who will sign a long lease of five years or more, as there is far less demand than years ago. If you do find tenants, they may not have any money behind them, then if they walk out, what do you do? It may not be worth pursuing them, although legally you are entitled to do so, meaning you are left out of pocket.

With residential property, the trend over the last 50 years has seen residential values increase dramatically (with the odd recession in between, but they recover well). There's also a huge shortage in housing stock, which has created the demand for rental houses and flats.

Recently, I tried to help a friend who purchased a new office building in 1990 for £1m. He asked me to look at it with a view to converting it into residential flats, as he said he couldn't let it out without parking facilities. The best I could offer him was £650,000. Although he's earned rent for many years on the property, its value has actually gone down by nearly half since he bought it.

Likewise, I bought an empty shop back in 1988 and let it out for £12,000 a year as a kebab shop. I finally got an increase in the rent two years ago, when I managed to get £15,000 a year. That's not a great increase considering I've owned it for 25 years! Years ago, I used to buy shops with flats above them. I would sell the flat off, getting most of my money back, and then let the shop out, but these days it's really not worth it.

There are exceptions to the rule and some property developers specialise in secondary commercial property. However, on the whole, I would not invest in commercial property – at least not initially.

It's also a lot easier to borrow money on residential property than it is on commercial. With commercial property, the bank will probably only lend you the money over the term of the lease. As soon as the property is empty, the value can plummet dramatically until the shop is re-let. You can take a bigger chance and buy a vacant shop and attempt to re-let it on a long lease, on a good rent if you can. But, in the meantime, you have empty rates to pay.

Houses vs flats

I've converted numerous houses, hotels, and maltings into flats over the years. I've also converted a number of other buildings into what I call 'vertical split houses'. These are sophisticated developments and so I don't recommend that you begin with developments like these immediately. What we're talking about here is whether it's best to buy houses to refurbish, or a converted flat – in both cases to either let or sell on.

The caveat to both of these options is that, if it's very, very cheap and there aren't any huge problems, then it probably doesn't matter which you choose. However, there are a few things to be cautious of.

The great thing about buying a house is that you are in total control of your own destiny. If it needs decorating, you can decorate it. If it's got a crack in the wall, you can investigate it yourself and sort out the problem. Aside from building regulations and conservation areas, you basically don't have to ask for anybody's permission to do what you want to do.

With a flat, it is totally different – as flats are sold **leasehold**. The point of being leasehold is that each flat shares the common parts of the building, such as the roof, the communal hallways, windows, brickwork, external painting and so on. Each flat pays a fair share of the costs through a service charge, which goes towards keeping the building in good order. This is only fair, as, otherwise, only one flat would be responsible for the roof – the top flat! For this reason, I have very rarely come across a flat that is being sold as freehold, but if you do come across one, don't buy it!

Leases

If you're buying a flat, be very wary of the length of lease left. If it has less than 80 years left to run, then most building societies won't lend on it. You can, however, apply to extend the existing lease back to its original length. For example, if it was a 125-year lease, you can apply to the freeholder of the property to extend the lease back to its 125 years.

There is a cost for this to be done, which is a mathematical calculation carried out to get to a fair price for the time extension. There are a number of chartered surveyors who specialise in these calculations. My advice is to seek out one of these if you are in this situation. They will also negotiate on your behalf with the freeholder of the property.

If you can't agree a figure, you can go to the land tribunal, whose final decision is binding. The freeholder cannot refuse to extend the lease. If they do, you can go to the land tribunal where the matter will be settled at no cost to yourself.

You now have far more control as a leaseholder than ever

before; however, make sure you look at the lease carefully as there may be restrictions. It may say you can't have pets, or you need permission before you decorate. It will definitely say that you need permission for any structural work.

It never ceases to amaze me how many flat owners don't seek permission before doing building alterations to their flat. If you're going to do building work to modernise a leasehold flat, you must get permission for that work *prior* to starting it, or at least check with your solicitor whether you need to get permission.

When you come to sell the property, the buyer's solicitor will ask whether you have written permission for any alterations you have made. If you didn't get permission, then you will have to ask the freeholder for retrospective permission, which they may not be willing to give. In fact, under the terms of the lease, they could ask you to put the flat back to the condition it was in before the unpermitted alterations.

Service charges and sinking funds

The next issue is the service charge, which is the cost of running the building, together with a sinking fund towards external maintenance when it's required. The sinking fund is a very important mechanism for looking after the long-term condition of a block of flats. It's a way of making sure that every year, a percentage of the service charge is put aside for the large jobs that need doing every five to six years, such as external redecorating. You need to be aware that any buildings over two storeys high must have scaffolding erected for external work, which has increased the price of external decoration enormously.

Under new laws, it is now possible for the residents of a block to manage it themselves. It is also possible for them to get together and purchase the freehold amongst themselves, as long as more than 50% wish to do so. The current freeholder cannot refuse the request. If the price can't be agreed, again the land tribunal will step in and, in these cases, they are very much on the side of the tenants.

I have personal experience of this as a landlord – having to sell the freehold investment on a block of 40 flats to the residents who owned their flats on long leases – as well as also losing control of the management in other blocks, even though I still owned flats in them.

If you're thinking of purchasing a purpose-built flat, there are normally less problems involved and it probably won't need as much refurbishment. However, most of the aforementioned issues still apply, so beware! Although I have purchased flats on a leasehold basis that need refurbishing, I much prefer to own the freehold for these reasons.

Purchasing new builds off-plan

Purchasing new build properties off-plan has become a very popular way of investing in property over the last 10 to 15 years. In most cases, you purchase them before they have been finished, or in some cases, before they have even been started. For what is probably a very small initial deposit – at a discount, you commit to purchase a property up to year and a half before it will be ready.

I've known many people who have done this and sold the property on before they had to pay to complete the purchase. They made a very good profit. However, I've also known people who have done the same thing but didn't manage to sell the property on before it had to be paid for. This got them into all sorts of financial difficulties.

So, unless you're a gambler, make sure you will have the funds ready to purchase the property when it's finished. The next factor is more difficult to judge – whether the property market will continue to go up, stay static, or go down in value during the year before you have to complete your purchase.

You also need to check whether there is a huge demand for the properties from the general public, prior to them being completed. If there is, then there will be a large demand and an opportunity to sell your property for more than you paid.

Another thing to check is whether it's part of a much larger scheme, where they will be continually building for the next three years or so. With all the mess and noise this creates, it will put off potential buyers.

If you're going to sell the property on, make sure the contract you are signing has a clause that says it's assignable. Your solicitor will be able to check this for you. This means you can avoid the stamp duty due on the property – because you are selling it on before you are buying it – which you would otherwise have to pay.

If this clause is not in the contract, you have to pay the stamp duty and your buyer will also have to pay the stamp duty, with no way of getting it back. Make sure your solicitor is strong and insists that the contract you sign is assignable in the first place. This will potentially save you thousands of pounds!

CHAPTER 8:
TYPES OF PROPERTY DEVELOPMENT

Earlier, I said that when it comes to property development, you need to be inspired by the project. You want it to keep your interest, whether it's renovations, refurbishments, rental properties, or letting out shops. So, in this chapter, we'll look at renovations and refurbishments, listed buildings, and where to buy. Later, we'll look at buying-to-rent.

Refurbishments

Now for the fun part! Buying to convert, or refurbishing existing buildings, has been the mainstay of my business for the last 35 years. From experience, I know it's very easy to think that a building won't cost much to convert or refurbish. You are likely to be optimistic, excited, and highly motivated to take on a project at this point. I don't want to depress you, or put you off, as it is great fun, but, in 35 years, I don't think I've ever had a project come in on time, or under budget. I've managed one or the other, but never both together, so be warned!

Of course, if it just needs decorating and a new bathroom, that is a very different scenario. When I say **full refurbishment**, I mean a complete renovation from the roof to the windows, the wiring, bathroom, kitchen, re-plastering, and so on. In such cases, you need to get a full schedule of works done, so the builder knows exactly what they are quoting on. That way, there's no arguments and each builder you ask for a quote is pricing it on the same information. This is known as quoting on a like-for-like basis.

To get a full schedule of works, you need a **building surveyor**. Never, ever use an architect for this job. They may well try to convince you that they can cope with the whole job, but while architects are normally very talented, nice people, who will do a wonderful job of designing and remodelling your project on paper, when it comes to the practicalities, you need someone a lot more hard-nosed to deal with the builders and other tradesmen.

A good, strong-minded building surveyor might charge up to 10% of the value of the job. If they do and they're good, then they are well worth the money. You don't want to be dealing with the builders on a day-to-day basis. Part of the surveyor's job is to value the work that has been carried out and to only pay if satisfied. I don't know of any builder who ever undervalued an interim invoice, so save yourself a headache – get a good building surveyor!

When you first have a look around the property, if you see that the building doesn't look symmetrical from the outside, or internally the doorways don't look level, or the building has any cracks in the brickwork, I recommend that you get a **structural engineer** to have a look at it, even if you've already made the offer and it's before you exchange contracts.

There are two types of structural engineers: the first type is too scared to cross the road because they'll get run over and the second type is more pragmatic, who will give you sensible advice on how to get past whatever problem there is. Over the years, I've learnt – to my cost – about the two different types. On occasions, I've had to get a second opinion, which has normally been very different from the first, more cautious one. However, if you find a good one and they still advise you not to buy, then please take their advice!

When it comes to refurbishments, ensure you get a good job done. If you just 'paper over the cracks', someone *will* notice and have a full survey done, so don't try to wing it! In the past, you could sometimes hide a crack with render, but nowadays everyone is far more cautious when purchasing. So, you need to make sure the property refurbishment is of a high standard.

Renovation tips

I could write a book on its own about renovations and, like any number of the popular TV shows, I could tell you that you should put coffee on, bake some bread and hang some nice curtains but, as you've probably realised, this book is about hard facts. There are plenty of so-called experts who will advise you on colour schemes and such like, but it's important to focus on the money first and foremost.

There are a few things that work very well when renovating and can be the difference between a property looking average or professionally finished:

- Although it might be very tempting, to reduce costs, never use second-hand materials of any sort, including kitchens and bathrooms.
- Ensure you finish everything to the best possible standard you can. Don't pick the cheapest items – always choose something of decent quality.
- If you can, always install a wet radiator heating system in gas, if not oil, although, having said that, electric wet radiator systems have now improved greatly.
- Make sure the painters have painted the cupboards inside as well as out, as many don't.

- Make sure all the windows open and none of them have been been painted closed.
- Make sure that all the lights have shades on.
- It needs to look sharp and clean – and be certain to keep to simple colours.
- Make sure the carpets have been hoovered and there's no carpet remnants left.

As you can see, successful selling starts with a **good finish**. If you're changing the doors, don't go for the cheapest. For a little more, you can get solid oak doors. It's the same with the door furniture; go for something of quality that 'clunks' when you shut it. You'll be amazed at how a simple thing like this makes such a difference. People's standards of how they wish to live have increased vastly over the last 20 years. Most people want the house to look like a show home, or a top hotel room when they move in.

Carpets are another area where people often go wrong. Put down underlay, which is very cheap, then you can put down a cheaper carpet. Potential buyers will think it's Axminster when they walk on it, but you'll have achieved the same feel at a fraction of the cost. Kitchens and bathrooms are now rarely carpeted, as attractive laminate flooring is much more desirable.

You have to make it as easy as possible to sell the house – so don't forget the **outside**. Make sure the garden is clean and tidy. Builders are a nightmare for not getting rid of their final rubbish, so make sure it gets cleared up immediately. Don't seed the grass – turf it, as it will change the garden instantly. Make sure the doorbells work, that the gate isn't rusty and put down new pea shingle or gravel; it's cheap and covers a multitude of sins. Check that the fences are renewed if rotten. Even if the actual fence isn't yours, if it looks a mess, ask your neighbour whether they mind you replacing it. Don't be stubborn just because it's not yours.

Specific renovations

If it's a **terraced** house, make sure there are fire walls in the attic, so you can't get through to the house next door. Also make sure it's very well insulated up there. In the past, many affairs were known to have taken place between householders, when they could just go up into the loft, walk along three or four houses, and then drop down to their lover's landing!

If the property has a **cellar**, don't get sucked into spending too much money on it. Whitewash it so it looks clean. The fact it might be damp doesn't matter, as it's below ground level. Market it as storage only and you won't disappoint any viewers. Some people invest in a waterproofing system for basements and cellars, commonly known as 'Tanking'. This is when the whole basement, including floors and all walls, are made completely waterproof. There are a number of systems on the market, most of which come with guarantees. Just make sure you read the small print carefully and ensure the work is checked as it proceeds, so there can be no argument in the future that the work isn't in accordance with the guarantee.

If the property has a **basement** with windows, you could consider making it into a habitable room. However, in my experience, giving people the ability to do it themselves later will give them the impression that you've missed an opportunity – when really, you've done the wise thing. If you do decide to convert, be aware that basements are very difficult to keep dry. Guarantees from companies that tank basements with a waterproof render need to be read very carefully.

If you're **rewiring** the property, make sure the electrician is fully qualified and gives you a certificate at the end of the job, which should be handed to your solicitor to put into the sales pack. The central heating boiler needs to be registered with the local authority and this also needs to be put into the sales pack, along with any other guarantees for kitchen appliances. You'll be amazed how many times we have lost guarantees on fridges, cookers and so on, so be methodical about these things.

Finally, once the carpets are down, get a **builder's clean** (which doesn't mean the builder does it, because that would be a complete mess!) Employ a professional cleaning company to come in and clean everywhere, including the windows – both inside and out. If, for any reason, it doesn't sell quickly, make sure you continue to keep it clean and tidy and remove any post.

Renovating a house to live in prior to selling

Many people like the idea of taking on a renovation project – the sort of job that may take two years to complete – with a view to living in it for a short period of time, before selling it on at a good profit, and then finding another one to do.

I always admire the energy, ambition, and positive outlook of these people regarding the challenge ahead. However, sometimes a little knowledge is a dangerous thing! As you know, there are a number of programmes on TV that often demonstrate how these projects progress – and the challenges and the dramas make great viewing. However, you don't want that to be you!

So, here are a few tips to make sure no TV producer will be using your property for a show! The first thing is make sure you have fully costed out the project first and have sufficient funds. Even if you're doing a lot of the work yourself, you still need to buy materials. You may also need expert help along the way – which costs money, too.

If you haven't got all the funds available, then prioritise the work to make the property liveable. To be able to obtain a mortgage, the property needs to be habitable – in other words, it needs a bathroom and a kitchen. If it has those two things, most building societies will lend you a percentage of the value of the property.

As the project proceeds, they will also top up the loan they have given you once certain jobs are done, such as a new roof, new windows, central heating and so on. This means you should be able to get stage payments out of the building society, which will no doubt be essential in order to complete the project.

One of the first things to check on any renovation property is that the roof is watertight, because without a watertight roof, you don't have a house to live in! You need to do the most important jobs first; the roof, damp-proofing, electrical wiring, plumbing, heating and windows.

You can leave the other jobs until later on, when funds are easier to come by, such as the garden and most externals. Unless you want to sell the property, it won't matter that it's not decorated, the drive isn't finished and the fences aren't up until later. I've seen so many people get in a muddle and do the things they like to do first, rather than things they should be doing.

When negotiating to purchase the property, assuming it's vacant, it's well worth asking whether you can exchange contracts with a delayed completion. This means more than the normal 28 days. This way, you may be allowed in to start renovating before completing; you could get the upstairs rooms into a habitable state, even if it means putting in a temporary kitchen and a new bathroom. Make sure the seller understands that you don't wish to move into the property before completionm – just to gain access in order to renovate.

Many people have a romantic notion of buying a mobile home, putting it in the front garden and living in it for nine months while working on the house. Let me tell you, there isn't much to be romantic about when you've been in it for three months, it's cold and damp and the shower isn't great. If you're living there as a couple, or with children as well, the novelty soon wears off, I can assure you!

My advice is quite simple; if you can get a few rooms renovated quickly upstairs, then you can live up there while you do the rest of the house. It's also an awful lot cheaper than buying a caravan for £20,000 or more and having to live in it for twice as long than you initially thought! There is enough stress when renovating a property, without trying to live in a caravan, with an 8ft × 6ft bedroom, and a shower you can't even walk into!

If the option of living on the first floor of the property is not a viable option, another alternative is to rent a small house or flat while you're doing the renovations. A final option is to live with your parents, or friends. However, make sure you know how long you're going to be there before committing to moving in as there's nothing worse than having someone outstay their welcome. Whether you're related or not, it can ruin relationships!

Listed buildings

I've renovated a good many listed buildings over the years, but it's not something I would recommend at the early stages of your developing career. Any issues you may have with the normal renovation of a house are magnified if it is either grade 2 or grade 2*. I've only ever done one grade 1 house renovation – but never again! Everything you do is totally and utterly scrutinised by the listed building officer – quite rightly too, however, as no doubt it's an important historical building.

I recently bought the old YMCA in Norwich, which is a grade 2*. I obtained planning permission for three town houses and sold it to a company that had never undertaken a conversion. They asked me to act as a consultant on the project as they wanted to alter the existing plan, changing it to six two-bedroomed apartments and one townhouse. I brought my team of experts in to make sure the project went smoothly, which it did. However,

I can't be everywhere, so my advice is please don't attempt to undertake such an ambitious scheme for your first project.

If you do decide to ignore my advice, then be aware that obtaining listed building consent is long and arduous, and requires a very good architect with specialist knowledge in listed buildings. Even then, there can be numerous meetings and negotiations needed with the conservation department of the council.

With a listed building, you are always having to compromise between the history of the building and the modernisation of it. It may be that you can't do everything you want to do in terms of modernisation. The listed buildings officer at the local authority has to give you permission to do so and, if they think it compromises the history of the building, they won't let you do it. So, don't assume you can modernise the building before you get permission.

Never, ever start to develop a listed building without the listed building consent in place. If you do, then an enforcement notice will very quickly be served on you and you'll have to stop work. You are also liable to be sued, as it's a criminal offence to not have this consent.

Conservation areas

Also check whether the property you are intending to purchase is in a conservation area. These properties are normally positioned within a historical part of the town and are often very popular, but they do come with restrictions. For instance, demolishing a property is very difficult and even being allowed to build or remove a brick wall could be a challenge.

You can check whether the property is in a conservation area on the local authority's website.

Many years ago, I owned a piece of land next to a block of

flats. In the past, the land had a building on it, so I wanted to apply for planning permission. There were some cherry trees on the site, so I asked my chap to remove the cherry trees and clear the site, which he did. I then had a notice served on me very quickly by the council stating that I had removed trees without permission. The trees did not have a preservation order on them, so I assumed I could just take them down; however, because they were in a conservation area, I still needed permission.

I ended up going along to what I thought was a council tribunal. However, when I got there, they had appointed a barrister and it was a court hearing! I had no legal representation, so I explained to the judge that it was a genuine mistake. She accepted this and only fined me £2000 as I'd already replaced the trees and apologised for my mistake. The maximum they could have fined me then was £20,000, and I'm sure it's even higher by now! So, be aware and always ask whether it's a conservation area or not before you buy.

The rule of thumb is that if the property is in a nice area, it's probably a conservation area—so planning is more difficult. However, it's nothing like the challenge of listed buildings!

Buildings with enforcement notices

You may sometimes come across a property with an enforcement notice on it. These are legal charges placed by the local authority, normally because certain works haven't been carried out to make the property habitable. If they're not put right, the local authority can legally go in and do the work, then charge the property owner for this – along with an extra amount as a penalty.

Enforcement notices usually get put on a property when the owner is absent, or has financial difficulties, so can't carry out the repairs required to bring the building up to standard. Or it could be that a structure has been built within the curtilage of the building, but the owner didn't have planning permission.

Sometimes, these notices aren't as bad as they sound. If you look to buy a property with one, ensure you can get the work done to lift the notice easily – without a fight from the council. Make sure you understand the work required by asking the enforcement officer, and that you carry out the work as stipulated.

The good news is that these notices may put off a number of potential buyers, but I wouldn't let it put you off – as long as you expect to do the work in a professional manner. Ensure you get the enforcement officer back to check the work after it's been done, make sure they sign it off as completed and that they register it.

There's nothing worse in this situation than getting a buyer and then having their solicitor tell you that there is still a notice on the building – when you know you've already had all the work done. This happens quite often, if the enforcement officer has moved on to another job and didn't lift the notice. It is **your responsibility** to ensure the notice has been lifted in the correct legal way, so always double-check that this has been done prior to any sale.

CHAPTER 9:
BUYING TO RENT

As a property developer, you might find that your interest is in buying properties to rent them out and building up a rental portfolio. In this chapter, I'll answer some of the common questions I get about buying property to rent.

Where to buy rental properties

I'm often asked where to buy for the best rental returns in the UK. An obvious answer to this question is to buy close to where you live, as it has a number of clear advantages. Knowing the local market and people, and keeping your ear to the ground, should give you a big advantage over someone from another area.

If you know about something that will change the area, such as new road redevelopment plans, this is something you can greatly use to your advantage. However, sometimes you can almost be too close to something and not see the bigger picture. You can often be biased, because you know the history of the area, so ensure you're being objective.

Over the years, I probably haven't bought enough property in my local area. I've always been willing to travel across the UK to get the best profit margins I can find. Sometimes I've pushed too hard, when I would have done as well by staying local and being stronger on my own patch. This is something that I've made an effort to do more of over the last few years.

However, it can also be worth buying rental property outside your area. It can be a challenge, but it can also be a successful venture. I don't want to put anyone off, because I have been successful in doing so, but what I will say is ensure you pick a very good area of the town to buy in. If you're looking to buy in a town that you're unfamiliar with, ask a taxi driver to drive you around for 10 minutes. In that time, you'll find out more from them than you'll ever get from an agent, and you'll certainly find out the no-go areas in that town.

Likewise, never buy properties on streets where that and other properties are boarded up, as it often means there is little need for rental properties there. If you buy it, refurbish it, and let it out, you'll probably find that the windows will be smashed in before you find a tenant. You'll end up in a vicious circle.

When it comes to buying rental properties out of town, people often say to me, "I don't want to buy property 200 miles away from where I live, because I will never see it". My answer is very simple: this is a business. If it's well-managed by the local property management company, why on earth do you want to look at it? You're never going to have to live in it, so does it really matter where it is in the country?

Capital growth, or rental yield?

Where you buy also depends on whether you're going for a high rental return on your outlay. If this is the case, buy in the poorer areas of the country, such as parts of the north. This will give you a brilliant return on your money. You can probably look to achieve 10% yield (financial return) in certain places. For instance, if you paid £100,000 for a property and received £10,000 a year in rent, that would be a 10% yield, which is great.

The downside is that you won't get capital growth in poorer areas. The better the rental return, normally the poorer the capital growth. In other words, if you bought something for £50,000 five years ago, it might only be worth £55,000 today, but you probably had a good rental return from it.

If you pick more affluent parts of the country, including parts of the north, you will find that your rental return isn't as good, but if you keep it for five years, your capital return should be much higher. For instance, if the property was worth £100,000 five years ago and is now worth £200,000, then the capital growth is £100,000.

It's interesting to note that rent paid by the local authority because the tenant is on benefits doesn't vary much between the north and the south, unless you're in London that is. Therefore, some of the cheaper properties have a much better rental return than the more expensive properties. If you're just looking for income from rent, there is very little point buying in the more expensive areas.

What to avoid

Unless you're incredibly rich to start with, or have found an amazing financial backer, there's also little point trying to find deals in London – as property prices are incredibly high. One of my biggest regrets is that I didn't buy in London 35 years ago, when I first started.

If you live in the south, it's difficult to comprehend, but there is often very little demand for rental houses and flats in certain parts of the country. So please check the market and do not buy in these areas.

There's an old saying: 'When buying horses, spend as much as you can afford, as good horses make good riders', and the same can be said of property. Why buy something that's going to be a lot of trouble? If a terraced house in Burnley is £20,000, there is a very, very good reason for it, and if you've heard about the property way down south, then it's certainly not a good deal.

Is it worth renting in university cities?

Over the last few years, there has been massive growth in the number of people going to university and an increase in the number of university places available. This has given property investors a great opportunity to get better yields on what would otherwise be pretty average property stock.

As student accommodation is often subsidised by student grants, loans, or the bank of mum and dad, the pressure on housing stock close to universities has made it a very attractive investment. This type of property often accommodates up to five people or so in one house. Students pay considerably more rent for a house than would normally be paid by a family, as each student pays for one room in the house.

Students pay a high level of rent in university cities and, even in a property recession, they still need accommodation, so it's always in great demand. This means your rental return can be very good compared to what you paid for the property. However, in recent times, universities have been building more purpose-built student accommodation. As such, it's very important that you check with the university how much accommodation is available and how much they need. If you contact them directly, they are always very happy to help and usually have a housing department within the university.

Of course, if your son or daughter is at the university, buying a house and renting out to their friends while they're at university, then selling afterwards can be a very clever move. Just make sure that the demand won't go down in those years and that your children have good friends, who will pay the rent and look after the property.

To ensure that student rent and costs are paid, I always ask for a parental guarantee. This is not just for the rent, but also to cover the condition of the property when it comes back to you. There can be no 'fingers crossed and hope for the best' attitude when it comes to renting a property, especially to students – even ones that you or your children know.

A word of warning: although you may consider that you're renting out your house, the local authority in that area might consider them to be bedsits, as you have a number of independent people living within the building who are not family members. This is very important, because they will insist that you adhere to more fire precautions than you would normally have in the building. It is always best to be cautious in these matters and check with the local authority to ascertain whether you need to provide a fire certificate.

You will find that the local fire officer is happy to come around and inspect the property and advise you correctly. There have been a number of cases of landlords being sued for manslaughter due to a tragic fire within their property, so don't let yourself end up in that situation.

How to choose tenants

Firstly, you'll want to choose a property management company. When it comes to choosing a company to look after your properties, I always do a lot of research, and ask numerous questions of the company before anything else. It's not a decision you want to get wrong.

Likewise, choosing tenants is a very difficult job. If you're not local to the property, you're unlikely to meet them. If you are local, I suggest you definitely arrange to meet any prospective tenants, as this could save you thousands of pounds and a lot of trouble and frustration in the long run.

Don't just rely on references. Just because the property management company you're using tells you they are acceptable and the references are good, it doesn't mean they are going to look after the property, decorate it, or keep it clean and tidy. I've got some wonderful friends, but not all of them are as clean and tidy as I would expect and most of them have got money!

If you can, ensure that the property management company checks the property every three months, rather than the standard six. If the property is not being kept in good condition, get rid of the tenants. They'll not only bring down the value of the property, but you'll end up undertaking remedial work to put things right again before it can be re-let.

It's all very well for the property management company to say, "Oh well, we have a deposit", but be aware that a deposit or one month's rent hardly goes anywhere, and you're never going to get any more money off the tenant, whatever the cost of the redecoration and repairs. You're not going to get a contribution from the property management company either.

My advice is that, if you've let bad tenants in, but subsequently realise you've made a mistake, get them out as soon as possible. It's better to have one month with no rent, than months of repairs and no rent.

One of the major things the management company must do is to inspect the property regularly. This may cost you more money, but in my experience, most property management companies offer great value for money. I normally agree with their fee structure, rather than trying to reduce it, because I want them to rent my property out before any of their other clients' properties and I want them to look after it as if it were their own.

Many years ago, when I was in my mid-20s, I started selling properties that I owned to the Granger Trust, which at the time was one of the biggest landlords in the UK; they had something like 25,000 properties. I could never understand why their rents were so competitive. I thought that if I ever owned that many properties, I would try to charge as much as I could all of the time, but of course I would have been totally wrong.

The reason they charged such competitive rents was because it was very important to them that they kept their occupancy rates as high as possible. What they didn't want was a lot of empty properties all around the country, which could get vandalised, become damp and so on. By keeping the rents competitive, it meant that less tenants moved out and, if they did, a new tenant moved in far quicker than if they tried to get top rental incomes.

The moral is: if you have good tenants, do your utmost to keep them in the property. If they move out because you put the rent up, any potential increase will be wiped out by the fact that you will have to find another tenant, even if it only takes you a month. Also remember that, as soon as the property is vacant, it doesn't look so attractive and could need redecorating, carpets cleaning, and so on. It's a bit like the saying 'Happy wife, happy life'. Happy tenants give you a stress-free life and the best rental return.

Should you get rental guarantees?

As its name suggests, a rental guarantee is an insurance policy that you can take out as a landlord for rental income protection. This type of insurance is often combined with legal expenses cover, to safeguard you against tenants who fail to pay the rent.

Obviously, there is a cost for such insurance, but if you

want to sleep well at night, without worrying whether you can cover all of your own costs each month, then such schemes are worth considering. Make sure you read all of the small print and completely understand what is and is not covered, and for what periods. Something that seems too good to be true usually is.

Is it worth managing your own properties?

If you're someone who doesn't worry too much, you can always manage your own rental properties. This was incredibly common in the past, when there were less landlords and certainly not as many property management companies.

There are clearly advantages to managing your own properties if you have the time, and you might do a better job than a property management company, which has hundreds of properties to manage. You can check the property as often as you want – a lot more often than a property management company would – as long as you give notice to the tenant.

Barging in without giving due notice is against the rights of the tenants – and rightly so. In the past, it was quite common for a landlord who wished to sell their property to show the buyer round the flat themselves, hardly bothering to knock on the door before letting themselves in with their own set of keys. On many occasions, I found myself, as a buyer, in an embarrassing situation with the landlord, when we found the tenant half-dressed, or asleep in their flat. If you rent the property yourself, it should go without saying that you need to be professional.

Another benefit of renting the property yourself is that you can also do any repairs personally, which is becoming more and more expensive through a management company, who, in some cases, I'm sure charge you for arranging the work. Likewise, finding tenants and vetting them yourself is better than trusting this job to a management company. Currently, there are number of ways you can market your rental property, such as through Gumtree, Facebook and other social media.

This may well sound very attractive, plus saving the commission you're paying to a property management company. However, a word of warning; it's all very well when things go smoothly, but when things don't – and they invariably do not – you are totally reliant on yourself to put things right, both legally and physically.

As a result, I actually see the involvement of a management company as a big advantage. They create a buffer between you and the tenant, which is not always a bad thing. It gives you time to get on and find more properties, or take more holidays and it means less pressure, less stress and no phone calls at 2am from a tenant who locked themselves out! If they are only charging you between 5% and 7% for doing the job, then it's better to employ a management company. Just keep an eye on what they are doing and don't let them have total control when work needs to be done – make sure you have full control over any money spent.

As in life, there is always a compromise. This might mean allowing them to manage the property once you have let it out, or finding you a tenant and you then managing it yourself.

Are holiday lets and Airbnb worth trying?

The idea of doing holiday lets, or Airbnb – which is the new phenomenon – has opened up the letting market even further. It makes letting your property out on a 12-month shorthold tenancy look rather tame and unexciting! However, sometimes there is nothing wrong with putting safety first and knowing exactly where you are financially on a monthly basis.

Of course, some properties wouldn't suit holiday lets, or Airbnb, because they aren't in a good enough condition, or an area where people want to go on holiday. They might not be close enough to the workplace for short-term commitments. However, if it does suit the holiday market, then you need to consider certain factors first.

The most important factor is how many weeks of the year you can let the property out for. Over the years, I've looked at doing this myself, but have always concluded that I can only guarantee letting the property out for 30 weeks of the year. The rest of the time, it may be let out, or it might not be. If it's not, you have to cover the empty rates and look after the building, which normally means keeping the heating on in the winter. In the end, I've always gone for safety first and let it for 12 months on a shorthold tenancy.

If you do want to let out your property for either type of short letting, you could manage it yourself through a website. These days, most people still use the traditional method of a holiday lettings agency for holiday lettings, but manage it directly online for Airbnb.

Holiday letting agencies are normally very well-organised and do a good job, but this comes at a cost, which is normally about 20% of the rental price. However, most letting agents aren't likely to tell you that they can only let it for 30 weeks of the year, as they are likely to be over-optimistic. There is also a lot of work involved, from checking people in and out to cleaning, laundry, and gardening.

Of course, if you're in a really famous holiday destination, you are likely to be able to let it out for considerably more than 30 weeks of the year! However, you'll be paying a lot of money for a property in such a popular area. This means that, even if it's let out for more than 30 weeks of the year, it's unlikely to show a very good return on your financial outlay, because you're having to pay so much money for the property in the first place.

If you'll be using it during the year yourself, then you can subsidise your costs very nicely rather than leaving it vacant for the rest of the year. I've heard that even Roman Abramovich rents his super yachts out!

Airbnb has become a phenomenon over recent years and a number of my friends have used it to rent out their home annex. They don't want to have someone living there for the whole year, but they're delighted to receive income for some of that period, especially when they're away themselves.

Some investors buy apartments and houses just to specialise in renting them out on a daily, weekly, or even monthly basis. For people who work away from home, it's a very viable and cheaper alternative, rather than living in a hotel room.

Of course, the shorter the rental stay, the more you can charge. So if you're willing to put the leg-work in for such lettings, then the return on your capital could be very good indeed. In other words, the amount of money you paid for the property compared to the income you can receive annually is great. In my view, it's a bed-and-breakfast you're offering without the breakfast!

However, like with holiday lettings, it's all very well if you can readily rent out the property for the majority of the year, but if it's for 30 weeks of the year or less, then you still need to look at the return you'll be generating.

With both holiday lets and Airbnb, there's no point in kidding yourself and looking at the gross rental return you're receiving. So, when you go to a dinner party and people tell you how wonderful it is, remember that having a property fully let on a short-hold tenancy for 12 months, with little hassle, is also very appealing. But, if it sounds too good to be true, then it normally is! You need to be honest with yourself and look at what the net return is after all of the costs. If the return still looks good, then I'm delighted for you!

Can I get financial grants for rentals?

Over the years, I've managed to obtain a number of grants from both local authorities and housing associations.These organisations sometimes have funds allocated to them – normally from central government – to financially support private landlords, who wish to improve their housing stock on the basis that they will continue to rent their properties out.

These grants aren't always available, but if you own or are purchasing a property that requires updating, it's well worth enquiring with the local authority initially to see whether any grants are available.They should also have information on whether any housing associations have funds available.

These grants can vary from money for roof insulation or a new central heating system to more comprehensive refurbishment of the property, including the roof and rewiring.

The best time to apply for these grants is usually at the start of the local authority's financial year, which is generally in April, rather than towards the end of the year when the money has all been allocated.

Normally, any grant is linked to you being able to let the property for a minimum of five years. If you want to sell it within that period of time, you have to pay some, if not all, of the grant back. So always check and make sure you know the facts before accepting any grant.

Many years ago, I took out a large grant on eight flats from a housing association, on the agreement that they rented the flats off me to put their tenants in for a minimum of five years, at a discount rent of 15% off the market rent. This was absolutely fine for me, as I got the properties completely renovated in return.

However, not only did I start to get complaints from some of the other tenants in the block about the behaviour of the housing association tenants there, but we also had a number of incidents where flats were flooded.

When I investigated these complaints and issues, I found out that the housing association had rented the flats out to recovering drug addicts, who had clearly fallen back into their old ways and were taking out the kitchens and bathrooms to sell for their habit, causing floods and enormous distress to other residents.

The good news was that they had to return the flats in the same excellent condition they were given them, five years later, but it wasn't much comfort to the other residents in the block. The moral of the story is make sure you investigate the grant better than I did on that occasion!

How to start and grow a rental portfolio

One of the easiest ways to start a rental portfolio is if you are already a homeowner. This gives you two very good options.

The first is to refinance your property by increasing the amount of your mortgage on your existing property, which will give you the deposit to put down on your first buy-to-let mortgage. Of course, it's very important to make sure that you can afford the increased monthly mortgage payments on the first home that you are living in.

It's also very important to make sure the property you're buying is in good condition, so you don't need to spend much money to let it out for a good rent. If you only have the deposit available to put down and no additional funds, you'll put yourself under pressure if you then need to find more money to refurbish the property.

The second way is if you're thinking of moving to a bigger house and you're selling your existing house. It makes perfect sense to let your house out instead, then purchase your new one, either out of additional funds that you have, or by mortgaging your first house and swapping it to a buy-to-let mortgage. Buy-to-let mortgages allow you to borrow up to 75% percent of the value of the property – as long as the rent has 150% coverage. In other words, if the rent is £750 per month and the mortgage payment is £500 per month, that would be 150% cover. However, don't forget that you have to pay for repairs and maintenance, a property management fee and probably taxes too.

If you're not an existing homeowner, starting a portfolio will be harder, as somehow you have to find the 25% deposit in order to purchase your first buy-to-let investment property.

We went through the various funding options earlier, but another idea if you're really struggling is to find a like-minded person who is also struggling to find the 25% deposit and purchase one together, each putting in 12.5%.

Over the years, I have had numerous business partners, all of whom I'm still on very good terms with and do business with today. However, you do need to be the right type of person to work in this manner – where you are jointly putting in the same money. You certainly can't both be control freaks!

Like all good partnerships, it's best that each of you have a particular role to play within the agreement. One might look after the tenants, rent and financial side, while the other keeps an eye on the repairs and maintenance. If you get on well, you might look for your next purchase together, but I'd give it a few months to find out first!

Once you've bought your first investment property, the next one should be easier. It could be that you've managed to save enough money from your job to put down a 25% deposit and get a buy-to-let mortgage on the second property. Or you might refinance the first property because it's gone up in value, enabling you to put a deposit down on the second property with a buy-to-let mortgage.

It could be that your family or another person is prepared to lend you the deposit, in order to share the uplift in the property's value and the rental income over the next few years. This allowsyou to get on and purchase more properties while the market is still rising. We'll cover what to do if the market drops in another chapter.

Of course, if you're fortunate not to have any mortgage on your current home and own it outright, or you only have a small mortgage, then you can probably afford to purchase three houses by refinancing your existing house. If the market is rising, then, after a couple of years, you'll probably be able to refinance those properties and purchase another two without putting in any more additional funds. You can continue doing that every couple of years until the market looks like it is starting to change.

CHAPTER 10:
WORKING WITH BUILDERS
& OTHER TRADESPEOPLE

When you're developing property, the quality of your builder and other tradespeople is really important. We've all heard horrific stories about them. So, in this chapter, we'll look at how to find and choose a good builder, the common things that can go wrong, and how to avoid these pitfalls.

Finding a builder

A good source of recommendations for a builder is from an estate agency that also does property management. This is because they continually need builders to repair and renew their client's houses. It is well worth speaking to them, and they are normally very happy to recommend someone who works for them. If you join a landlord association, or similar, this is also a good way of finding out who the good builders are.

Personal recommendations are always the best way of finding a builder. However, be cautious! Don't pick a builder who you have met socially and struck up a rapport with. You're not looking for a friend – you're looking for someone to enter into business transactions with.

It's always best to find **one builder** who then organises the rest of the trades required. That way, the builder is responsible for the complete job. Some people try to save money by employing a builder for the building work only, opting to coordinate all the other trades themselves, such as plumbers and electricians.

In my experience, you are best to leave the builder to organise the whole job and coordinate all the trades themselves. They may charge you more than what the plumber would charge you directly, but if it's not done on time, it's the builder's responsibility. Plus, you only have one person to deal with, rather than five.

If it's a bigger job, then it's essential to have a building surveyor hold your hand through the process. For a smaller job, you are on your own, because it's not worth employing a surveyor and they probably wouldn't be interested in taking on the work on anyway.

Choosing the builder

When you've found a few builders, ask them for quotes. Make sure you write down **everything** you want done, so each builder is pricing up the same amount of work on a like-for-like basis. Otherwise, you will have a distorted view of the prices.

When it comes to choosing who to go with, don't always go for the cheapest quote. Have a look at the other work the builder has done and try to talk to the owner to see whether they did the work within the agreed timescale. Always remember, interest is accruing on the money you have borrowed – so even if one builder is slightly more expensive than another, if they'll do it competently and quickly, it's worth it. Quicker means less hassle, less stress and more profit.

Never settle on an open-ended agreement, day work, or suchlike. Even if you think you know them and trust them, this leaves you open to all sorts of problems and disagreements. You wouldn't cross the road with your eyes shut. So never enter into any agreement with a builder not knowing what the final costs will be. The key to all of this is to finish the job as **quickly, efficiently**, and **economically** as possible. You will not achieve this if you have any disagreements whatsoever with the builder.

Common problems

In this section, we'll look at some of the common problems that can occur when you hire builders, and some easy ways to avoid these pitfalls, or resolve the problems if they happen.

Too many jobs

In my experience, most builders are decent and want to do a good job. The biggest problem is that they don't like saying no, or turning work down, because they have to pay their staff whether they are busy or not, so they are always worried about keeping them busy. As such, the strategy of most small-scale builders is to have three jobs on at any one time, where each client doesn't know that there are two other jobs running concurrently.

You can't really blame them, as they don't know when the tap is going to be turned off, as it were. However, when you get to your property to check on the work and find there is just one builder working, it can be very frustrating —as time is money. The longer it takes to get the job done, the less you will make because of the interest payments, so you need to continually drive the job forward.

To avoid this, give the builder a timescale to complete the job. This timescale needs to be *agreed* with the builder, rather than *dictating* it them. You need to create a working partnership to your mutual benefit. The sooner the builder finishes the job, the sooner they can move on to another one – although they might have already started it!

Paying the builder

Assuming you have been given a fixed price by the builder that you're happy with, make sure that you don't overpay them on a monthly basis. Some builders will try to overcharge for the work they have done early on, which helps with their cash flow, but it leaves very little incentive for them to finish the job at the end.

By the time the job is finished, make sure you still have at least 15% to 20% in-hand to pay them, which you can give them upon total completion of the job. When I say completely finished, I mean *completely*, including everything being clean and tidy. The most important thing at the end of the builder's contract is the snagging list, which we talked about in Chapter 5.

This is where you check each room without the builder and write down anything that still needs to be finished properly. Don't start the snagging list until they confirm they have finished. Give the builder the list and ask them to work through it. When they say it's done, go back and check. If things still aren't right, write out another snagging list. Don't forget to ensure the builder has registered the boiler with the council, and that you have received all of the relevant guarantees from them. Only when it is all completed to your satisfaction, should you pay the final amount.

Allowing for extras

Whatever the agreed price for the building contract, allow an extra 10% for any genuine extras there may be during the renovation. It's very difficult to be completely accurate on a fixed price. For instance, when the builder pulls off the rotten skirting boards, or uncovers the original fireplace, they don't know what they're going to find underneath. Some discoveries may put the value of the property up and make it more saleable, but always set aside 10% extra to ensure you can happily cover the full cost of the works.

Getting the job done on time

Unfortunately, the builder will inevitably be late in finishing the job, so if you agree three months, allow four and a half months without telling the builder. That way, although it will be frustrating, you will quietly have a smile on your face that it's being done in the time you expected!

Also, don't give the builder any excuses for being late, such as changing the specification yourself halfway through. You are better to take a little longer getting the specifications absolutely right *before* starting, rather than changing your mind later. Not only will it give the builder the excuse that it can't be done on time, but it will cost you. As the builder is already on-site, you can't get anyone else in to make the changes, so they can charge more.

One trick I've used over the years to get the job done on time is telling the builder that the carpets are being put down a week earlier than they actually are. You never have to admit that you've done it, because they will never be ready the week earlier, but it gives them a push, so hopefully they are ready the week after – when the carpets are actually booked in. You can tell the builder that you've done them a favour by putting the carpets back a week.

Finally, be thankful for builders in the UK. A friend of mine recently went to France to do a large fencing contract for a lady who'd moved there with her horses. My friend did the fencing work in nine days, although the local French fencing contractor had wanted six weeks. The French builder decided to leave work a day early for his four-week annual closedown in August, leaving her with no running water – work that he could have finished if he hadn't left early. Instead, he just said he would do it on his return to work on 1st September! Having heard that story, I've become a lot more grateful for UK builders!

CHAPTER 11:
WORKING WITH SOLICITORS
& ESTATE AGENTS

Some people will have you believe that it doesn't really matter who your solicitor is, as it's purely legal transactions. Let me tell you that a poor solicitor, or terrible licensed conveyancer will lose you a lot of money over the years, by not acting quickly enough, not saving a transaction that could be saved, giving you negative advice, or being lazy. Choosing a good one is vital to your success as a property developer.

Throughout this book, I've emphasised the importance of getting a good estate agent on board. When you find a good agent, they not only take you smoothly through the current deal, but they are a great source of future deals. So, in this chapter, we'll look at how to work with estate agents, solicitors, and accountants.

Choosing a solicitor

Licensed conveyancers specialise only in conveying property through the legal process. Solicitors deal with different aspects of the law as well as property. It really doesn't matter whether you choose a fully qualified solicitor, or a licensed conveyancer who concentrates purely on property transactions. When choosing either, make sure they work full-time, that they are not about to go off on maternity or paternity leave, or a long holiday, or embark on job sharing. Ask the question and make sure that whoever you choose is good!

You need to choose a solicitor or licensed conveyancer who you can meet in person. It needs to be someone who will keep you fully advised **all the way** through the transaction by email or telephone. They also need to have the authority to make decisions on the spot, rather than having to go through a manager.

I have used the same solicitor for 25 years or more. He emails me on a Sunday and has even exchanged contracts for me while he's lying on a beach in Barbados. He is generally available to me 16 hours a day. I'm not expecting you to find someone who is prepared to do that for you, but you need to make sure the person you choose is interested in what they do and is committed to giving you the best possible service.

Do not just go for the cheapest. Make sure you like them, and they get on with you. Don't choose one who has only just qualified. They won't have the experience required – let them make their mistakes with someone else, not you! Your relationship with your solicitor really needs to be a partnership. Only bother them when you need to, and via email rather than telephone if possible. Then, if you do telephone them, they will realise it's important.

Conveyancing factories

Lately, there is a real fashion for choosing a cheap conveyancer, from what I call 'conveyancing factories'. This is a new method of property conveyancing, where unqualified people initially do the basic work, then it is checked at the end by a qualified person. They were set up to deal with high volumes of transactions.

However, this means that you don't get the same person dealing with your case every day. They work within a computer framework, so there is no personal interaction – you can't even speak to them on the phone. I strongly advise you not to use one of these firms! They may sound very cheap, but there's always a reason for it, so its really not worth using these companies.

Some of the larger corporate estate agents have set up these companies, or have a financial agreement to recommend them to their clients. If you're put under pressure to use a solicitor the agent recommends, do some research first. Find out where they are based and how they operate. You can always ask the estate agent whether the clients who have used these companies would recommend them to someone else.

Choosing an estate agent

As I mentioned earlier, if you've purchased a property through an agent and you are now selling it, then it's the done thing to give it back to the *same agent* to resell it for you. This helps to ensure you continue to get deals from them, and it's really the unspoken word in property dealing. However, that doesn't mean you have to be weak with them!

A good agent should automatically progress the sale for you and proactively deal with any problems. If they don't, then chase them up. Getting deals over the line is never easy, so be pleasant, persuasive and flexible with them.

If you didn't buy through an agent, then you get to choose who to sell your property with. In this case, you need to choose a good agent. To find one, look on Right Move and see who has the most properties for sale, as a good agent sells a lot. Don't be concerned if the agent no longer uses paper advertising, as this went out with the ark! It's all about being online.

You might want to choose an agent who does open house marketing. This is a modern way of marketing your property. The property is marketed for two weeks prior to the date of the open house. The intention is that you get as many people around as you can to create some competition. Not all agents like to undertake this form of marketing, but it can be very successful within a town or city. The trick is to not let anybody view the property before the open day. They will often try various excuses, like they can't make the day because it's their daughter's birthday, but if they're keen, they will turn up!

Sales progressors

Once you get your property 'under offer', the real work starts. At the estate agent offices I own, we have a team of sales progressors whose sole job is to work with the solicitor on your behalf, to get the deal through as quickly and as smoothly as possible.

Some agents realise the true benefit of these sales progressors. If you get to choose an agent to handle your property, try to find one that has such people in their team and ask for a weekly update from them. You can then liaise with the solicitor if anything isn't being done quickly enough.

Avoiding common pitfalls with estate agents

Please do not contemplate using an online agent. First of all, you have to pay an upfront fee whether they sell your property for you or not, so you could be wasting your time and money. Secondly, they are unlikely to give you a genuine price on what your house is worth, because they just want to get you to pay the fee upfront. Whether they sell it or not is irrelevant to them. Because they already have your money, there is no incentive for them to do any more.

Getting a buyer is just the start of the process. A good

traditional agent, with a sales progression team behind them, will work day and night to get your property completed, because if they don't, they get paid nothing.

Avoid choosing young and inexperienced negotiators – unless you've heard that they are extremely talented and good at what they do. If you're new to property development, you really need an experienced agent to help you through it. Always go for the manager if you can; don't be fobbed off here. Don't pay any upfront fees for advertising, or other ancillary items that the agent may suggest, as they are really not necessary.

Make sure you don't sign a sole agency agreement for more than 4 to 6 weeks with one agent. This way, the agent is kept on their toes and will try to get you a sale within the contract period, which is what you want – time is money. If they don't, then you can always take it off the market with them and seek another agent. However, don't place the property with more than one agent at the same time, as the agents will have no incentive to sell it for you – remember, you want your agent to be loyal to you.

Choosing an accountant

Finally, it's extremely important that you have the full financial facts regarding tax at your disposal. So, if you don't have an accountant, I suggest you find one immediately and ask their advice on whether or not you need to form a property company to purchase your properties. When choosing an accountant, make sure they don't drive a new, expensive car, as that's your job, not theirs! You want a cautious person who asks you sensible questions and gives you sound advice.

As there is an allowance for unearned income, they may advise you to purchase your first property in your personal name, rather than a company name. However, it's important to seek a professional accountant's advice here.

The government websites are also very useful, especially regarding how much stamp duty you should be paying on your property purchases and any tax you need to pay on rental income. Everybody has to pay tax on their profits, so make sure you take good advice before you start investing or trading in property. That way, you and your accountant can plan your financial affairs going forward. As I always say, "*fail to plan, plan to fail*".

Hopefully, by now, you have chosen a really good solicitor, a great agent, and a trustworthy accountant who can make all the difference in helping the sale go as smoothly as possible.

CHAPTER 12:
BUYING AND SELLING
AT AUCTION

Buying and selling at auction has become far more popular in the last 10 years and is why I invested in Auction House UK, along with my business partner, during the 2009 recession. The business has grown from seven franchises to over 40 and is now the leading auction business in the UK, based on the number of properties sold annually.

The world of auctions

Around 30 years ago, I used to go to auctions and know quite a few people there, and we were all property dealers. In fact, if you got there late and missed the lot you wanted to buy, you could quite often ask the person who had just bought it whether they would be happy to sell it to you for a small profit.

There were a few common tricks used in the past when buying at auctions. For example, people used to ask a question in the auction room before the lot they were interested in came up, such as whether there was a report on the structure of the building – suggesting that there could be a structural problem with it, even when they knew there wasn't. At our auctions, we don't allow anyone to ask any questions once the auction has started, so we have stopped that game!

Nowadays, most of the auction rooms are filled with people like yourselves who are looking to invest in a house or to renovate and resell it, and I'm absolutely delighted you are there. Numerous property shows such as *Homes Under the Hammer* have opened up the market to many more people, giving them the confidence to be able to buy at auctions.

The great thing when buying at an auction is that the legal packs are all online, including the search. This means your solicitor can very quickly check that everything with the property is as it should be before the auction. You can also view the property beforehand. With the confidence that you have taken legal advice, viewed the property, agreed a price for any building work and have the funding in place, then you are all set to purchase at auction.

The guide price

Remember that the guide price is purely that – a guide price. If, for example its between £100,000 and £120,000, then the reserve is likely to be halfway between the two. Of course, this can change depending on interest in the property and how many times the legal pack has been downloaded, as we use that and the viewing days as a guide to the level of interest in that particular property.

However, don't get put off if there have been numerous legal pack downloads by different solicitors. I agree it may mean lots of people are interested in purchasing and may turn up to bid, however it doesn't always happen that way, so make sure you turn up at the auction.

Bidding

When the bidding starts, try to relax. I still get tense when I'm bidding and that's after 35 years! Always let someone else do the running in terms of the bidding, i.e. let them bid first. When bidding, be decisive, but don't keep waving your hand at the auctioneer, as you might end up bidding against yourself.

Wait until the auctioneer says two things: one is "It's here to be sold" – in other words, it has reached its reserve price. The second is when the auctioneer says, "Going once" – at that point, make sure you are very visible to the auctioneer and get your hand up in the air. With a bit of luck, it will dishearten the person who thought they were buying it, as you are a fresh new bidder.

I have a rule when buying at auction: my limit is where I can make a least 25% profit out of the deal. If I have to, I allow myself to pay another 5% above my limit. If I still don't get it, I know I've given myself every opportunity to buy. Never, ever get overexcited and bid too much for property, as there will always be another one.

People now bid online and also on the phone from their home. However, I always advise you to go in person as you never know what's going on otherwise. Always turn up at the auction yourself, as it's great fun and you can soak up the atmosphere. You can also meet like-minded people and make many new contacts.

Never allow anyone else to bid on your behalf. There are lots of stories of people who have done that – and their friends have bid on the wrong lot. They ring up afterwards in excitement saying they got it for half of what they expected to pay – only to find out that they bought the wrong property. Take the responsibility of bidding yourself.

The winning bid

The thing I love about buying at auctions is that when the hammer comes down on your bid, it is yours. No seller can change their mind. Once the property has been knocked down to you, you'll be approached by an auction runner, who will ask you to come to the desk. There, you'll sit down, sign the contract, and pay the 10% deposit. There will also probably be a buyer's fee. Make sure you check what this is prior to the auction. So many people forget to do so. This is normally between £200 and £1000 upon signing the auction contract. However, it can be any amount that the auctioneer wishes to charge, which goes towards the costs of running the auction.

There are some property dealers who only check the auction to see which properties have *not sold,* then make an offer after the auction has ended. If you wish to purchase a property after the auction, there is no reason why you can't say to the auctioneer that you're willing to purchase it, but that you want your solicitor to go through all the legal papers first before you are prepared to sign the contract.

After the auction has taken place, the last bid made on an unsold lot will be published. However, don't be fooled into thinking you need to bid over that amount to buy the property. The significant fact is that it did not sell in the auction room. The auction is over and no one purchased the property, so don't be embarrassed to offer lower than that figure. Remember, no auction house gets paid if the property is not sold, so they are keen for you to purchase after the auction too! This is a good way of purchasing a property as you know it is available and on the market to be sold.

Buying and selling at auction is so smooth, that I always try to have a property in one of our auctions to sell. It's a great way of keeping the cash flow going. If you buy a property very cheaply at the auction, you can always put it straight into the next auction, without spending any money on it whatsoever, and see whether it sells for a quick profit.

CHAPTER 13:
TRADING IN A RISING
OR DROPPING MARKET

When you've been buying and selling property for a while, you come to realise that markets fluctuate on a monthly basis – they are never static. It's important to know what to do with your properties as the market changes. In our estate agency offices, we find that December and January are traditionally quieter than April to July (avoiding August, due to holidays). So, if you are looking to buy or sell, consider that different months affect sales timescales. In this chapter, we'll look at what to do in a rising or dropping market, and what to do during a property recession.

Trading in a rising market

A rising market means that the property market quickly rises in value. Property that normally might take a while to sell starts selling very quickly. More and more people want to purchase at this time, because they are concerned that, in the future, they won't be able to do so. This causes a shortage of property to buy, which pushes the prices up higher.

I often say that even my dog Ivy could make money in a rising market, if she could use her paw as a signature that is! There is very little skill involved in jumping on the bandwagon and doing what everyone else does – buying in a rising market. In that market, everybody *can* make money, because all you're relying on is inflation. You don't need any skill whatsoever.

However, it can go wrong. Good intuition will lead you to get out at the right time, but very few people ever do so, either because of greed, or being scared of not being *in* the market. Having common sense and sticking to your game plan will see you though these times.

In the mid 80s, a great friend of mine started out decorating houses. Within a few years, he owned a £1m country house. He managed to do a number of risky property deals that are possible in a hot, inflated market. So, he thought everything he touched would turn to gold. I remember him showing me that he had £1m in the bank.

However, when the recession came, he lost everything, eventually selling his furniture in order to get the rental deposit together for a flat. He never saw fear in anything he did, but if you keep taking risks, like a very fast car driver, eventually you will have a crash. Some people bounce back, but, in my experience, very few learn the lesson.

Trading in a dropping market

A dropping market is when the property market prices start to reduce, most often because of an oversupply, a lack of credit being available to purchase and/or a lack of confidence in the economy – usually because of a national recession.

In the UK, property recessions come around periodically. This usually happens when the market is so inflated, that first-time buyers can't purchase because they have to borrow between four to six times their net income per annum. 'Property recession' is a term that no one likes to hear in the property world.

Property recessions happen for a number of reasons, such as a financial crisis. Sometimes they happen because of a general recession in the country, meaning less people have jobs, so less people have the confidence to purchase a property, or move to a bigger one. The banks and building societies then have borrowers who can't afford to pay their mortgages, because they have lost their jobs, so they have their properties repossessed. This leads to banks and building societies losing confidence in lending and reducing the amount of money they wish to lend on property. They also make it more difficult for buyers to obtain mortgages, as they increase the criteria required to be accepted. For instance, they may reduce the percentage they will lend on a property from 70% to 50%.

All this means that there is an excess of property on the market, because less people are buying, and less people are able to get mortgages. In turn, the prices of properties reduce, eventually to the point that people will start to return to the market and so overall confidence will grow.

If anyone tells you that a property recession isn't going to happen, or could never happen again, be absolutely clear that this is not true – it *will* happen! In my career, I have survived three property recessions so far.

Getting out of the market

I'm not saying you shouldn't invest when the market is rising, because it is a great time to purchase. Also, there's nothing wrong in being brave and borrowing as much as you can on your investments to keep buying, but don't get too greedy. You are far better to get out of the market earlier than other people, rather than hanging on and losing everything.

Be willing to jump off the merry-go-round before everybody

else does, because as soon as everyone gets off, the property prices drop dramatically. However, knowing when it will stop is difficult. There are plenty of so-called experts who don't get it right, including the banks.

In the past, new car sales in the UK have been a great barometer for the property market. When new car sales reduce from the year before, it is a good sign that prices in the property market will follow.

Here are a few signs that may help you make the right decisions at the right time:

- When building societies and banks start lending 100% first-time buyer mortgages.
- When you see new house builders offering to trade in someone's existing property in order to buy a new one.
- When first-time buyers can no longer afford to purchase a property and have to get a mortgage of up to around five times their annual salary (although this is becoming less relevant than in the past, as parents often help these buyers out).

You will find that most agents are in denial about a looming property recession, because they don't want to believe what might happen. If they're young, they won't have seen this happen before, so won't know what to do, or how to advise you correctly.

So, what do you do when you believe all or some of these signs are appearing? The answer is to quickly finish any properties that you are currently developing and make sure they go on the market at competitive prices. If they don't sell quickly, reduce the sale figures again. And don't buy any more for the time being – as the saying goes, 'never catch a falling knife!'

Having survived three property recessions with various levels of success, I can assure you that, when the recession really bites, you need to reduce your prices **more than anybody else** in order to be able to sell. When the market starts falling, you need to react quickly and reduce your prices before other sellers. Within 10 weeks, your reduced price will have been caught up with and you will need to reduce it again if you haven't sold the property by then.

I hear many people say that, because they couldn't sell the property for what they thought it was worth, would only be getting their money back, or would lose a small amount, they decided to rent it out instead. If you purchased a property in order to refurbish and sell it, **stick to your plan**. Changing your mind and renting it out is just burying your head in the sand. For starters, the market will probably continue to get worse while it's rented out, so unless you're willing to wait a number of years, you won't get your money back. You need to release the funds by selling the property in order to reinvest, whether immediately, or when the market starts to improve. If you don't, you will have no opportunity to make more money, as your funds will be tied up. Cash is king!

By taking my advice, you will be ahead of the game. If you own multiple properties, then I suggest you sell some of them in order to reduce the borrowings on the rest of your stock. That way, even if 30% is wiped off the value of your remaining properties, your mortgages will still be a lot less than the value of your properties. **Don't do any trading in a dropping market** – wait until the market bounces off the floor and there are signs that things are starting to improve.

When to get back in the market

The exciting thing is, that by doing this, you will be in a great position when things start to pick up again! There will be numerous bargains to be had and you'll be able to take full advantage of them because you got out early! By the time a property recession is over, there are few people left in a position to purchase property quickly.

One of the first signs of stability is that new car sales will pick up. Traditionally, they are one of the first things to come back when the market is in recovery, before property does. Then it's time to get yourself back in the market aggressively, if you can. Property prices will be low, and you'll be able to step back in, before everyone else realises it is safe to do so.

Don't berate yourself

The property market is like a large ship in that it takes a long time to slow down, stop, and turn around. Sometimes, you might be better to forget about the whole market for two years, but if, like many property developers (me included), you are a 'deal junkie', you'll always be looking for that next big deal. With good intuition and an ounce of common sense, you'll probably find it's there to be had.

However, it's not always possible to make a good profit out of every property transaction. Show me a property developer who has never lost a penny on a property deal. The trick is to realise when there is a problem, accept you've made a mistake and stand up to be counted. Get out of it as quick as you can. Your first offer in such an instance is probably going to be your best offer, so take it and move on.

I never worry about the mistakes I make. Firstly, there aren't too many of them! I never dwell on them and I don't worry if I've missed a deal and someone else has gone on to make a lot of money out of it. Don't lose confidence, – there will always be another deal!

CHAPTER 14:
REDUCING
THE AGREED PRICE

Sometimes you'll put an offer in on a property, but then you need to reduce the price. Never feel bad if you feel you have agreed to pay too much for a particular property. The most important thing is that you **do not proceed** with the sale at that price.

There are numerous reasons why you might have agreed to pay too much. You might have simply got carried away. It could be that the market is dropping, so you need to reassess the price you agreed, or even consider pulling out altogether. You might have found things wrong with the property and have a very justified reason for renegotiating the price. It could be that you're just greedy and want to make more profit. There's nothing wrong with any of these reasons. So, in this chapter, I'll tell you how to get the price reduced.

Don't avoid the problem

If it's an agent who you work with a lot, or wish to strike up a good relationship with, clearly this won't be the best start. In this situation, don't ignore the situation – face up to it and handle the fact that you want a price reduction head on. If you don't answer the phone to your agent, or you make your solicitor ignore the agent's emails and phone calls, you will acheive nothing, and will simply ensure that the agent never deals with you again.

The best thing to do is to just be honest with the agent. Explain why you feel the price is too high. Knowing agents as I do, they are likely to work as hard as they can to save the sale and to reach a compromise between both parties. They may not like you quite as much as you thought they would, but if you can agree a compromise on the price, at least they are likely to work with you again.

Clearly, you don't want to put an agent in a very difficult position at the last minute, if you already work together. However, they can always 'put the blame on you' when they speak to the seller. At the same time, if they do arrange the reduction, you are even more likely to work with the agent again.

Reasons to reduce the price

We've all agreed to pay too much for a house, got a bit overexcited, and then decided we need to reduce the price. It could be an issue with the survey, or the search might have brought up something you didn't know about. It might even be that you find the vendor is desperate to sell it, or any host of other problems. If you can find anything to use to bring the price down, do so. Property dealing is a business, and all property developers will do well to remember this.

If there's a lot of people chasing a deal, sometimes you might be better to offer more than you think it's worth in order to get a contract and get in control of the deal. Once you've done that and undertaken your research on it, you might find there's a very plausible reason to reduce the price.

How to get a price reduction

The trick is to be absolutely adamant that you're going to walk away from the deal if you don't get a reduction. Don't reduce the price to the extent that it is ridiculous though. It should be disappointing to the seller, but not so low that they will go back to square one with another buyer, when they could have your money immediately. Make it just enough of a reduction that they still want to sell the property to you and move on.

Ideally, it should still be tempting enough for the seller to continue with the sale. Knowledge is power, so if you can find out how much they paid and how much they owe, you can price the reduction accordingly. Virtually every property in the UK is now registered with the land registry, so you can go to their website and glean a lot of information about a property that is registered, or ask your solicitor to do this instead. You can also find out when the property was last sold and how much for, through property websites such as Right Move and Zoopla.

Going straight to completion and avoiding the seller having to wait for the money is a good tactic if you wish to reduce the price, because you are giving them the opportunity to receive all the money for the property immediately, rather than just exchanging on the normal 10% deposit and waiting ato get the balance in a month's time, which is the average time between exchange and completion. This is obviously a great benefit to the seller.

If they come back with a compromise

If they come back with a compromise, which is what I normally try to do if I'm in their position, don't be totally inflexible. Initially, they need to think you won't compromise, but in reality, you're dealing. If the deal stacks up at the reduced price they are suggesting, then its definitely worth considering – even if you go back to them with another figure yourself. The fact that they're talking to you and not blanking you is good. You clearly won't be on their Christmas card list, but I'm sure you've got plenty of friends anyway!

It's business

Over the years, I've been asked many times how I live with myself, for being a property developer with a reputation for being hard-nosed and business-like. How do I feel when people think I'm being unfair, unreasonable, and ruthless, or taking advantage of a situation? My answer is quite simple, I've got plenty friends. I sleep like a baby, I have investors and banks to satisfy – and they always send me Christmas cards!

Reducing the price at the last minute happens all the time. It's all part of the business. A fellow property investor once told me about a time that he bought a large house, with a plan to convert into several smaller homes. They were grade 2 listed, and the more he looked into the deal, the more complicated it became. The vendor unwisely informed him about a tax bill he had to pay on January 31st and that he needed a completion before that date.

Over the following three weeks, the vendor then proceeded to phone him 50 times. On 30th January, the investor told the vendor he was ready to exchange and complete immediately, rather than the vendor having to wait a month to complete. However, after thinking about the number of phone calls he had received off the vendor, he reduced the price by one thousand pounds for each phone call. The vendor called him every name under the sun, but he replied "That's absolutely fine. I completely understand, but if you change your mind, let me know". The lesson here is, however rude the vendor is to you when you deliver bad news, always keep cool. Don't fall out with them – give them the opportunity to ring you back and agree to the new price.

The next day, the vendor rang back to say that the investor was still a b*****d, but he would accept the new price if they could complete that day. Now, some of you reading this will be appalled at what he did. However, the investor thought he was a bit soft and could have reduced it further! This is business.

I would also stress that many people purchasing a house to live in also reduce the price at the last moment, not just investors. Sometimes it's because of the survey, or valuation. It has been done to me hundreds of times. Whether such knowledge condones your actions or not is for you to reconcile with your own moral compass.

Clearly these tactics are at the sharp end of the property industry and will not be divulged to you by any TV property presenter, but you're reading this book to find out what happens in property dealing. Whether you use these tactics or not is entirely up to you.

If you want to pull out of the deal

Sometimes, you need to pull out of the deal completely. In this case, it is really best to just bite the bullet and say, "I've made a mistake and I don't wish to buy". Across the industry, approximately 30% of deals that are agreed by the estate agent do not proceed, so it won't be the first time they have to deal with this situation, or the last, whatever they may say.

You just need to hope that they will deal with you again. There is certainly no point in buying just to keep the agent happy. They might make a bit of a fuss and even try and make you feel bad or guilty, but you really must ignore it. There will always be another deal, so learn from your mistakes and move on – just look at it as a free lesson.

CONCLUSION

I hope you have enjoyed reading this book, and have managed to take something positive from it. Being involved in the property industry is a very exciting way of life! I hope I've helped you to clarify what you are interested in and what you would like to buy.

If you haven't purchased yet, but intend to do so, I hope you take some of my ideas and thinking on board. However, if you've already purchased, then I hope you had a good deal and that my advice helped you in renovating, letting, or selling – and will help you get an even better deal next time.

If you haven't decided whether to take the plunge into the world of property dealing and investing, I hope I may persuade you to do so. It's a great life and there's never a dull day.

Every day, I wake up not knowing what might come across my desk, who will offer me a deal, and whether or not I'll take it. Tomorrow might bring me the best deal I've ever had. Today, I've already had a meeting at 7am and agreed to sell a building I've just got planning on to convert into three houses.

If you enjoyed this book and want to learn more advanced concepts, look out for my second book on property development. It will give you a thorough insight into undertaking larger property transactions, as well as obtaining planning permission, plus building and converting large buildings into residential accommodation.